JESUS ACCORDING TO...

Contemporary answers to Jesus'
haunting question
"Who do you say that I am?"

by Edd Anthony, OFM

St. Paul Books & Media

Library of Congress Cataloging-in-Publication Data

Contemporary responses to Jesus' haunting question, "Who do you
   say that I am?": Jesus according to Mother Angelica ... [et al.]:
   interviews / by Edd Anthony; editing by R. Stephen Almagno
   and Theresa Frances Myers.
      p.   cm.

   ISBN 0-8198-3954-X

   1. Catholics—United States—Interviews. 2. Spiritual life—
Catholic authors. 3. Jesus Christ—Influence. 4. Jesus
Christ—Knowableness. I. Angelica, Mother, PCPA. II. Anthony,
Edd. III. Setticase, Christine S. IV. Almagno, Romano Stephen.
V. Myers, Theresa Frances.

BX1407.S66C66   1992
232-dc20   92-34767
                                                                      CIP

Printed and published in the U.S.A. by St. Paul Books & Media
50 St. Paul's Avenue, Boston, MA 02130

St. Paul Books & Media is the publishing house of the Daughters of
St. Paul, an international congregation of women religious serving
the Church with the communications media.

      1 2 3 4 5 6 7 8 9   99 98 97 96 95 94 93 92

Dedication

One of the qualities of a genuine friend is to have him share your dreams and to believe with you in the dark. For the past twelve years, I have been blest with such a friend in Curt Johnson. Curt has shared the vision of Franciscan Canticle and struggled with me through its difficult beginnings. He has contributed to its growth with his award-winning photography and his administrative skills. He is always there with a word of encouragement, his generosity, and his warm personality. With gratitude and appreciation, I dedicate this book to Curt, a genuine friend.

Edd Anthony, OFM

Contents

Preface

I have always been interested in the perceptions and images which others have of Jesus Christ. I believe that by sharing our intimate moments with Jesus, we help each other to grow on the journey of faith. While sharing these ideas with my friend, co-worker and producer, Sr. Christine, FSP, we conceived the idea of this book. After many months of patient work—interviewing, transcribing, editing—we hope that the honest spiritual sharing of the thoughts and experiences of some of these great spiritual leaders of our era will be a source of inspiration and courage to all who read them.

Edd Anthony, OFM
Director of Franciscan Canticle, Inc.

Franciscan Canticle, Inc., is a community of men and women artists who share the vision of Saint Francis with the desire to promote the Word of God through the use of their gifts and talents. Francis urged that artistic ability in people be used to praise God. Experiencing nature and society, the Franciscan artist reflects upon life in the challenging, creative, and supportive atmosphere of the community. Here, there is time and space to touch upon the indwelling God and to reflect this presence back to society. Through Franciscan Canticle, we hope to convey to the world the beauty and wonder of God by using the artistic talents given us in service to others.

For further information contact Franciscan Canticle, Inc., 13333 Palmdale Road, Victorville, CA 92392.

Acknowledgments

A special thank you to all those who gave so generously of their time and talent to the creation of this book. Especially to Christine Salvatore Setticase, FSP, the project coordinator, R. Stephen Almagno, OFM and Theresa Frances Myers, FSP, editors, and to Fran Ericson and Lynne Jagemann, OSF, for transcribing and typing. And to all those individuals interviewed in this book, for giving their time and allowing themselves to be questioned on a very personal matter—their relationship and journey with Jesus.

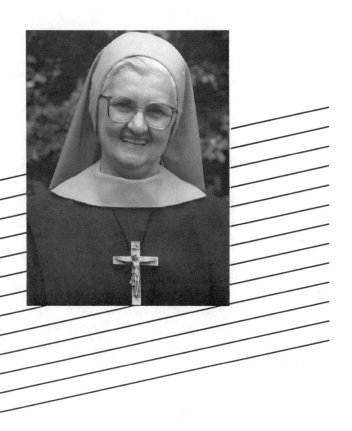

Born and raised in Canton,
Ohio, Mother Angelica, PCPA,
is known throughout the United
States and in many parts of the
world through her extraordinary
ministry with the Eternal Word
Television Network. A member
of the Poor Clare Nuns of
Perpetual Adoration, Mother
Angelica lives in the monastery
of Our Lady of the Angels in
Birmingham, Alabama.

MOTHER ANGELICA

• • •Q *Mother, would you first say something about the Eternal Word Television Network? What's it all about?*

• • •A Well, in this country we're all very concerned with diets and health. We all know that no matter how much food we eat, we sometimes lack some essential vitamins. We need to take vitamin supplements. Now, the average Catholic today has a great need to supplement his/her spiritual life—Eternal Word Television Network is meant to be that supplement. At EWTN we try to suggest how to live with God according to the Gospel. We try to present the beauty of the Church's teachings in such a way that they become a way of life, something livable and lovable. You see, many people know about God—but they don't know God. Nor do they have an experience of God, a living relationship with God.

• • •Q *And if Jesus were a guest on one of your programs, what would you ask him to talk about?*

• • •A I don't know if I'd want him to say too much. I think his presence on a live show would radiate ultimate, absolute love—and that would be breathtaking to everyone in the audience. I think that he would grab them before he ever said a word. That's what happened when he was walking on the earth. That's why sinners—Peter, the possessed man, Magdalene, Matthew—were attracted to him. I would invite him to look at the audience. And I think that his eyes, his face, his being would open our hearts to him.

• • •**Q** *I like that. And in your own spiritual life, how do you experience the presence of Jesus? Who is Jesus for Mother Angelica?*

• • •**A** Well, Jesus is many things at many different times. I experience him as lover, bridegroom, teacher, Lord, Messiah, Savior—the various aspects of his life as they fit into my life at a particular time. I do my best, imperfect as that is, to live and to see Jesus in the events of the present moment. If the past is a part of the present moment to teach me something, then it becomes the present moment. It may be that the future, in planning this or that, or in making a particular decision is a part of the present moment.... Sometimes it is not an easy thing to do, but my spirituality is entirely bound up in the effort of finding him in the present moment.

• • •**Q** *And do you have a favorite text from Scripture that kind of centers you in that? Or one that gives you courage or comfort?*

• • •**A** Yes. There is a passage in Corinthians which says that we, with our unveiled faces, see the image of Jesus as if in a mirror. And through the work of the Spirit of the Lord we are turned and transformed into that very image, from one degree of glory to another. I would like that passage (cf 2 Cor 3:18) put on my tombstone, because for me it epitomizes the entire thrust of the soul towards God. Right now, I reflect his image so dimly. But, as St. Paul says, as time goes on we grow brighter and brighter until we become the image we reflect.

• • •**Q** *Mother, I know that Eucharistic Adoration is an important part of life in your monastery. How does that fit into your personal relationship with Jesus?*

• • •**A** The adoration of the Eucharist and veneration of our Lady *is* our life, our duty, and the essence of our vocation. In fact, our monastery is built in such a way that we are never more than a hundred feet away from the Eucharist. It is that Eucharistic Presence that gives life and hope to the present moment. His Real Presence means that, when I go out into the world and come home again, I'm able to see him face to face; I sit, kneel, or whatever, and tell him what happened today. If I'm dead tired and I can't think, and I feel as if my body is falling through the floorboards, then I can just be miserable in his presence. I look at him and I wait upon him. I listen; if he doesn't speak, then I'm happy just to be in absolute awe in his wondrous presence.

• • •**Q** *You mentioned veneration to our Lady, can you say more about Mary in your spiritual life?*

• • •**A** Our Lady is my protectress. She guides me and pushes me in the right direction. When I stray, or make little detours, she obtains the graces I need to know her Son and love him all the more. I'm convinced that love for Jesus in the Eucharist and for his mother are the two things—the only two things—that will save the world today. The greed, the hatred and selfishness, the terrible situation that our country and the whole world is in...none of it will ever be resolved until we realize that the world was created by God, for God. It's our duty to show the world that the only solution to its problems is the Prince of Peace.

• • •**Q**   *Are there other attributes of Jesus that especially appeal to you at this moment in your spiritual life?*

• • •**A**   Well, I think the thing that attracts me to the Lord at this moment is his total, absolute, unselfish and unconditional love. It's very difficult for the average person to accept that love of Jesus. Either they have a slightly Jansenistic view of God—we must be perfect, make all the right decisions, and do all the right things before he loves us—or they have the opposite view, which is presumptuous—God is so compassionate and loving that I can sin, do this or that, and its all right. Instead, I must try to accept Jesus on his terms, not mine. My motives are not always the most pure, but his are ultimately, absolutely, totally pure and unselfish... with all of himself given to me freely. And this is not in spite of myself but because I am in need. I am weak, and he knows that unless he upholds me in the present moment I will fall miserably.

• • •**Q**   *Why do you think it is so difficult for people to accept that free love of Jesus?*

• • •**A**   In this world of New Age and cults, positive thinking and all the rest, we dislike being in need. We want to be somebody, to be able to handle everything, make all the right decisions—and we draw away from God. But in reality the greatest thing about Jesus is that he always responds to my great need of him. When persons run from me, when I'm in need, when I'm sick, when I'm down, when I fail, he runs towards me; he is near me and he holds me up.

• • •**Q**   *When did you first have an awareness of that love and know that Jesus was walking with you?*

• • •**A**   Well, until my eighteenth or nineteenth birth-day I didn't know Jesus at all. I think the awareness really came about when I was healed through the intercession of St. Therese, the Little Flower. Prior to that, I didn't know God. You see, my childhood was very miserable. In those days, being a child of divorced parents was not the most popular thing—there was a certain aloneness. I think I was the only child of divorced parents in the school, and it was difficult. We were hungry. We lived in cold, rat-infested apartments. Life was a matter of survival, not religion or devotion. So I didn't know God that well. But then I was healed, and I knew one thing for sure: that in order to heal me, God had to know me and to love me enough to say, "Rita, be healed." It was then that I knew there was a God, a Jesus, a Savior, a Lord, and that he loved me— which is something I never experienced from anyone else.

• • •**Q** *Did that realization have an immediate impact on your life?*

• • •**A** Oh yes. My finding God was because he touched me, just as he had touched so many poor people when he walked the earth. I knew for the first time that the Creator of all people and things was a personal God who knew me, chose me, loved me, and healed me. And that realization meant everything.

• • •**Q** *Is that when you decided to become a religious?*

• • •**A** After I was healed I began to make the Stations of the Cross every night after work. And one evening, as I was kneeling before the altar of Our Lady of Sorrows, I knew—just as sure as I was kneeling there—that I had a vocation.

• • •**Q** *And how do you nurture and maintain your relationship with Jesus? How do you keep the wood on the fire and burning?*

• • • **A**   Well, I keep it on the fire because I'm so aware of my own misery. I'll tell you what happened to me once when I was being given a Mother of Mercy Award in Toledo, Ohio. The affair was a big wingding and there must have been two or three thousand people at the luncheon. It took four people to introduce me, and as the last person began to speak (and I was getting bored), I looked out into the room, and the whole thing suddenly disappeared! I saw an incident from when I was nine or ten years old...it was an ice cold night and the rats—and I mean sewer rats—were eating through the floorboards of our ground-floor apartment. One rat ran across the floor and turned and looked at me, and I looked back at him just absolutely petrified. Then it scurried away. That whole scene came back to me, and I heard our Lord saying: "Look, Rita, no matter what they're saying about you, remember where you were."

So, when I got up to give my talk, I said: "Well, I thank you for this award and for all you've said. But let me share with you a little experience that I just had as that young lady was introducing me." And I told them the whole thing. There was a great silence—then tears and everything else.... That's how I manage to keep the fire going. Once you know, and keep in mind, who you were, what you are, who you could become, you stay close to the fire. But the moment you forget, or believe all the beautiful things people say, that is disastrous.

For many years a religious of the Sacred Heart, and now wife of Judge Robert H. Bork, Mary Ellen is a teacher, author and lecturer. A graduate of the Catholic University of America (MA in theology), she also studied at Manhattanville College and Siena College. She currently serves on the Executive Committee of the Washington DC Chapter of the Catholic League for Civil and Religious Rights, is on the Board of Directors of the Notre Dame Catechetical Institute in Arlington, Virginia, and is an active member of the Catholic Campaign for America.

MARY ELLEN BORK

• • •**Q** *Mary Ellen, you've had such a varied background, first a religious of the Sacred Heart, now married to a prominent judge and living somewhat in the public eye, when did you really become aware of a personal relationship with Jesus in your life?*

• • •**A** Well, it all started when I was a child. I can remember going on vacation to Lake George in upstate New York. My uncle, a Franciscan priest, would come and stay with us. I would get up early on those summer mornings and go to Mass with him. During the day while he prayed his Office he'd explain to me what the Office was and we would talk about the Gospel. It was from that time that I really developed a great love of prayer. I think that I have a natural attraction to prayer.

• • •**Q** *What about your early school years? Did you attend Catholic school...?*

• • •**A** Yes, I went first to the Sacred Heart Academy and then to a Sacred Heart College. During those years I came to understand and love the devotion to the Sacred Heart, and that has influenced my thinking both about prayer and Christ. I remember a time when I was praying quietly in the high school chapel—I think I was a junior—and I experienced a moment of incredibly great joy. Looking back I think it was a real experience of God, his consolation and his presence. It certainly turned my thoughts toward religious life.

• • •**Q**   *And is the Sacred Heart your image of Jesus today?*

• • •**A**   Well, I don't have a strong physical image of him, although from time to time when I'm praying over the Gospels I will think about his physical image. I sometimes think about the expression on his face, the look in his eyes, and the strength of his presence when he was teaching on the hillsides, or when teaching the beatitudes.... When I think of Jesus, I sense his presence as being very strong and wise. I see him as the teacher, having a presence one would take note of and feel peaceful with.

• • •**Q**   *What other aspects of Jesus' personality appeal to you?*

• • •**A**   Besides his personality as a strong teacher, I think that he had a sense of humor. I imagine that he was a person who had definite feelings and ideas about things, but in a perfectly balanced way...neither too emotional nor too narrow. His compassion, a quality that shines in the Gospel texts, tells me that he is someone who immediately made people feel comfortable. I see Jesus having an affirming presence, and I see him as being very positive. All of those qualities appeal to me very much.

• • • **Q**   *And which Gospel text is the most comforting or most challenging for you? Are there any passages that you find yourself returning to in prayer?*

• • •**A**   Well, I love the text where Jesus says, "Father, I thank you that you've hidden these things from the

wise and the clever and revealed them to little ones"
(cf Lk 10:21). For years I've found great consolation in
that text. It's something that I can pray over many
times. It makes me think about God, the Trinity, and
exactly what the Father had in mind when he sent the
Son to be with us and to teach us. It also counsels an
attitude of humility.

I think the most challenging text is when Jesus
said, "If they have rejected me they will reject you" (cf
Lk 10:16). We're certainly living in a culture where that
rejection quickly becomes a reality if we choose to take a
strong stand on certain moral issues.

• • •**Q** *You certainly must have felt that rejection during
the difficult time of your husband's Supreme Court nomina-
tion! What helped you through that experience?*

• • •**A** We came through that intensely negative
period with no bitterness and with a sense of having
been protected. I felt as if we were surrounded by the
shield of faith; a shield that warded off the darts of the
evil one. My husband and I were also strengthened by
the prayers of people from all over the country. People
called from almost every state in the union, from all
religious backgrounds, to tell us that they were praying
for us...some even had all night vigils. It was an extraordinary outpouring of supportive love and care.

• • •**Q** *During that time didn't you also have a strong
experience while praying the Our Father?*

• • •**A** Yes. For three or four months after the nomina-
tion ordeal I had a very hard time praying the Our
Father. Each time I'd get to the line "forgive us our
trespasses as we forgive those who trespass against us,"
I just couldn't say it. I was finding it difficult to forgive
some people who were involved in my husband's

hearings, and I had to really pray for a spirit of forgiveness. In time I did get the grace; there finally came a day when I was able to say the words and I knew in my heart that I meant it. But it took awhile.

• • •**Q**   *Have there been other moments when you experienced a strong sense of the Lord's presence?*

• • •**A**   I remember an experience that happened after I had made a thirty day retreat. I returned from the retreat with an inner vision which lasted for several days and made everything new. It was as if I were seeing the people with whom I lived and the people I was teaching with new eyes, in the light of faith, and recognizing how beautiful they were as children of God! Of course we believe that, but we don't always go around thinking about it at every moment. It was as if I were able to remain in that vision and awareness. Every once in a while I think about that awareness and remember it as a great grace.

• • •**Q**   *Can you share with us other experiences when Jesus touched your life in a unique way?*

• • •**A**   Well, in the winter of 1976, while I was teaching at the Doane Stuart School in Albany, New York, one of my students was in a car accident. The young woman was in a coma for a couple of days and then died. We all went to the funeral at a small Presbyterian church in a tiny village north of Albany. During the ceremony—which consisted mostly of readings from Scripture—I remember having a profound experience of how thin the veil is that separates this life from the next. It's hard to describe exactly, but it was like a glimpse into eternal life—as if I could reach out and kind of put my hand through that veil. It was a sense of how close God is, how close he was to that student and to her family.... Every time I go to a funeral I recall that experience.

• • •Q   *Was that while you were with the Sisters of the Sacred Heart?*

• • •A   Yes, I was with the sisters for about fifteen years.

• • •Q   *But at a certain point you felt God calling you into a form of a lay ministry—which is really what you are now living and doing?*

• • •A   Yes, but it wasn't all so clear at the start! I would say that it evolved slowly, and that it has only been in the last several years that new opportunities have opened up for me.

• • •Q   *Haven't you started a Spiritual Classics reading group?*

• • •A   That's right. About four years ago, eight women friends of mine started a small group called Spiritual Classics. We meet once a month and read from the spiritual classics...most recently we've been reading St. Augustine, and it has been a wonderful experience. When we come together, we open with a prayer and then one of us leads the class. Towards the end of our session we pray for all manner of special intentions. Spiritual Classics has been a marvelous time of learning and sharing our faith as well as a means of supporting each other.

• • •Q   *Mary Ellen, what are some of the personal prayer methods that you practice in order to foster and express your relationship with Jesus?*

• • •A   Daily prayer is essential—and I do pray every day, preferably in the morning from fifteen to thirty minutes, more when I can. I try to say both the morning and evening Office, and, time permitting, I also take the Gospel of the next day and try to prepare for that by reading a couple of things: the Jerome Biblical Commentary, or a section from a booklet that comes out from the Word of God community. I also have a spiritual director and meet with him regularly. I go to Mass several times a week, and several times a year I try to make a short retreat or day of recollection. I also try to keep up regular spiritual reading. I actually do some of that in connection with my speaking obligations.

• • •**Q** *You're asked to speak on so many different topics, if Jesus came back to earth, what subjects would you like to see him deal with, perhaps even on prime time television?*

• • •**A** Well, that really is quite a question when you think of the influence that people on prime time television have! I think I would love to hear him speak as he did to the apostles on the road to Emmaus...explaining the meaning of Scripture. I think that would appeal to a large audience. It would be electrifying and I think it would touch many hearts.

A graduate of Fordham University, Dr. Ronda Chervin is wife, mother, professor, author and international lecturer. Currently an associate professor of philosophy at St. John Seminary in Camarillo, California, Dr. Chervin served as a consultant for the United States Bishops' pastoral on women.

RONDA CHERVIN

•••Q   *Ronda, when you come into God's presence, the presence of Jesus, how do you see him?*

•••A   Well, I have a very clear image, which is a mixture of Rembrandt's famous head of Christ, El Greco's head of Christ, and what I saw in Zeferelli's *Jesus of Nazareth*. Zeferelli's Christ really speaks to me, especially the scenes where he holds the face of Mary Magdalen—I identify with her very much. I picture Christ's face as absolutely pure, and yet passionate. I see Christ staring at me, and I see myself scrounging around like a little sandpiper on the beach, going a mile a minute. And then Jesus grabs me and says, "Be still, and know that I am God." So I make use of that image. Very often I sit and pray with pictures around me; art is very important to me.

•••Q   *And how would you picture Jesus' personality?*

•••A   Utterly compassionate...that's the image that always comes to mind. And it's the strong compassion of an El Greco Christ. I also see him as full of pity—some people may think the word pity is negative, but I don't see it as negative. I see myself, and others, as being such incredibly wounded and battered creatures—even if we pretend all is well—that we are desperately in need of Christ's compassion. And no matter how much we fail today, he looks at us with this gentle, absolute love saying: "Come back to me; come to me."

• • •**Q** *And when you read through Scripture, which words do you find most comforting?*

• • •**A** The text "Come to me, all you who are heavy laden..." (cf Mt 11:28-29)—because I have a basically melancholic disposition. Often I feel burdened, and I'm glad God lifts me out of it. I find that, if I go to him, Christ is always ready to help me and give me his peace.

• • •**Q** *Which words of Jesus challenge you the most?*

• • •**A** The text "Be you perfect..." (cf Mt 5:48). I can be an irritable, complaining and angry person—sometimes I just find the daily petty things irritating—and so I'm obviously a very imperfect person. I would like to be like a living flow of patient love..., so that text is very challenging for me.

• • •**Q** *So, as an active and sometimes angry and imperfect disciple, how would you describe your personal relationship with Jesus? Do you see him as teacher, rescuer, friend...?*

• • •**A** I think of him as lover. Lacking a father image (my father left when I was a child) and having no brothers, I searched for fulfillment in romantic love relationships. But I have found in Christ the utter fulfillment of everything. The whole mystical tradition of Christ as lover (in the Song of Songs, for example) appeals to me. And I experience that as a very I-Thou relationship every day in Holy Communion—I see that as the lover wanting to come right into the body of the beloved.

• • •**Q** *Ronda, when did your relationship with Jesus become a conscious part of your life?*

• • •**A** Well, I was an atheist as a child and I thought of everything religious as pure superstition. Still, I was drawn to images of Christ—especially to Dali's Christ, which I had purchased and hung in my college dorm. My friends wondered what an image of Christ was doing on my dorm wall! Later, I saw a picture of the Last Supper which fascinated me and drew me into an experience that culminated later, when I went on a European tour of Catholic art—I only went on the tour because I was bored by the prospect of spending the summer in bars! While in Rome we went to the Vatican Museum, and there I saw the Raphael tapestry, "The Miraculous Draught of Fishes." While I was looking at it, the face of Christ suddenly became alive, and I became aware that he was divine—so I came to Christ's divinity before I believed in God! The next day we had an audience with Pope Pius XII. I saw the Pope's face close up as he was blessing the sick, and I had the same impression as when viewing the Raphael tapestry: I could see that the head of the Church had the same expression as Christ, and that the Church was beautiful. With that, the doors were opened for my conversion. It was a very startling and strong experience.

• • •**Q** *What happened next?*

• • •**A** Well, as a philosophy student my primary interest in Christ was in the area of truth. So, for the longest time I focused on the Church and Christ as truth, and it took me quite a while to realize that Christ was love as well as truth. It was only with the Charismatic experience that I began to experience Christ as love within me...not as something that I had to stretch for, but rather as something always right within me.

• • •**Q**   *Ronda, can you tell us about any special moments when Jesus truly touched you, times when you were absolutely aware that he was there for you?*

• • •**A**   Yes, one experience of Jesus that I'd like to share comes from being the mother of three and the grandmother of three—and I'm referring to labor pains. The birth of a baby is one of the ways in which family people, aunts, uncles, everyone—even if they are not actually going through it—can see within one minute the most agonizing pain possible, followed by the greatest joy. And it seems to me that such an experience, such a personal experience of the crucifixion and the resurrection, is for many people an experience on the natural level wherein they can deeply identify with Christ.

• • •**Q**   *That's a beautiful and really earthy experience of resurrection! Do you have other examples from your everyday life?*

• • •**A**   Well, I think many times we experience Christ's love simply through another's forgiveness. I say that because I tend to feel rejected a lot. Once the feeling of rejection was so strong that I felt overwhelmingly desperate...it was very painful. In the midst of that pain I went to a monastery to pray, and Jesus sent me a direct vision of his beautiful face. In my heart I heard these words: "Am I not more beautiful than any person?" And it was a very deep experience of letting go of an addiction or idol worship of a human person. A human person can give only a tiny part of that love which Christ has for us—really, it's only Christ's love that can heal. Looking into the mirror of his absolutely loving eyes, you see your own reflection and you feel beautiful.

• • •**Q**   *Ronda, from your own experience, what would you say is important in the spiritual life for people who tend to feel rejected or unlovable?*

• • •**A**   I think that people who have experienced rejection have a real need for regular contemplative prayer—a time when they are open to receive the love that Christ has for them. And they will know that love is real because they will come to prayer utterly distraught, falling apart, knowing they can't get out of whatever they're in, and they will be helped and healed. They will know that it was something supernatural—something coming from Christ—because by themselves they were unable to scramble out of the pit they had been in.

• • •**Q**   *How do you nurture and foster your own relationship with Jesus?*

• • •**A**   Well, daily Mass is the staple of my spiritual life, and I've learned that from being a Benedictine Oblate. I also read the lives of the saints, because they're people who struggled with so many things. Another thing would be cultivating a regular prayer time. I'd like to have the consistency of a daily hour of prayer divided into two periods, but given the demands of my life and duties I can't always do that—so I often pray in the car using Christian music tapes or the Rosary. And spiritual friendships involving conversation and correspondence are also very important to me. As a very intense person, I have a great need to be in the company of people who will actively inspire me. And, happily, God has sent so many canonizable saints into my life. I feel very blessed by the memory and presence of these saints.

Fr. Harold Cohen, SJ, has served on the
National Service Committee of the
Charismatic Renewal and also works
with the Right to Life movement.
Working in radio since 1981, he is
presently on the staff of Mother
Angelica's Eternal Word Television
Network (EWTN). In 1985 he started
his own television ministry and
currently has programs on EWTN as
well as on other cable systems in this
country and around the world.

HAROLD COHEN, SJ

• • •Q *Father, you're so active in the TV apostolate, if Jesus came back to earth today and spoke on prime time television, which topics would you like him to address?*

• • •A Well, I think I would like him to speak about his great love for us, about his Father's love for us, and to remind us of the way to follow him. I'd like him to remind us that we have to repent of our sins, to fast and to avoid materialism. I'd love for him to preach again the Sermon on the Mount.

• • •Q *And what do you think Jesus would look like? The Gospels give us everything from the Good Shepherd to the righteous Jesus turning over the money changers' tables....*

• • •A I think my favorite image is that of the Sacred Heart with his arms extended. I also like the picture that comes from the revelations given to Sr. Faustina—Jesus as Divine Mercy. I feel that is a special revelation for our day and I try encourage people to look into it.

• • •Q *If you had to describe the type of person that Jesus was, what would you say?*

• • •A Well, I'd describe him as the most wonderful person that you could ever meet. The most loving, kind, merciful.... At the same time, I'd describe him as one who loves you enough to point out your faults and who will always draw you forward; one who loves you as you are, but who is helping you to stretch and to grow into what he wants you to be. Jesus is a person whose personality is never fully captured, there are so many sides to it. We're always getting new insights into who he is.

• • •**Q**   *And how do you picture Jesus in your own prayer?*

• • •**A**   I think of Jesus as friend; he is my best friend. I see Jesus as merciful Savior—his mercy, his love and mercy, are the things that most appeal to me.

• • •**Q**   *Father, when would you say that your relationship with Jesus became a meaningful, living part of your life?*

• • •**A**   My father was a non-practicing Catholic and my mother was a non-practicing Episcopalian, so I was in the seventh grade before they got around to sending me to catechism. But it was when I made my First Communion, and later, while a student at a Jesuit high school, that I came to a personal relationship with the Lord. At the end of high school I entered the Jesuits and my relationship with Jesus became even more meaningful through daily Communion and by reading the Gospels and the wonderful *Life of Christ*, by Archbishop Goodier. I must admit that after ordination, when I got very busy and didn't pray as I should, my relationship with Jesus didn't cease but it did cool. It was through the Charismatic Renewal that it deepened again.

• • •**Q**   *So was it the Charismatic Renewal that kind of revived the relationship?*

• • •**A**   It was. I'd say that after the Eucharist and my religious vocation, the greatest grace I've ever received was that of the baptism of the Holy Spirit.

• • •Q *Would you tell your story of the milk and the chocolate?*

• • •A Well, one night I made chocolate milk for myself and one for a fellow Jesuit. I poured chocolate syrup into a glass of milk and handed it to him. Of course, all the chocolate went to the bottom and he just looked at it. Then I said, "Gary, you've got to stir it up." That's like baptism in the Spirit. The Holy Spirit is in us, but he's not permeating us as he would like to. And when he begins to permeate and penetrate us, as the chocolate does to milk when it's stirred up, then we experience the baptism in the Spirit, or a new fullness in the Spirit, and our whole life changes. That's really what the Lord wants to do, to stir things up within us so that the Spirit is not just sitting, but is really alive in us.

• • •Q *And now, having experienced that "stirring up" of the Spirit, how do you nourish your relationship with Jesus?*

• • •A In addition to my other prayers, I like to talk to Jesus daily in an hour of prayer before the Blessed Sacrament. Even if the hour is broken up, half an hour in the morning and half an hour at night, I still try to do it. I usually pray the Divine Office and the Rosary. I firmly believe that consecration to Mary's Immaculate Heart and praying the Rosary are ways leading to greater fidelity in our relationship with God. I also like to find a book that I can read prayerfully and quietly. Right now I'm reading *The Fire Within*, by Thomas DuBay. Those are some of the ways in which I try to nourish my relationship with Jesus. Then, too, there is the tremendous privilege of the daily celebration of the Eucharist, with some time spent in thanksgiving.

• • •**Q**   *Father, which Gospel quote has come to be the most comforting or most challenging for you?*

• • •**A**   The Scripture quote that means the most to me is John 15:5, "I'm the vine, you are the branches. Whoever remains in me, with me in him, bears fruit in plenty, for cut off from me you can do nothing." I find that very comforting in that it speaks about the union with the Lord that we should have, and how that union is to bear apostolic fruit. As for the most challenging text, there are a number of them. For example, Ephesians 3:20, "Glory be to him whose power, working in us, can do infinitely more than we could ask or imagine." Or Mark 11:22, "Have faith in God. I tell you solemnly, if anyone says to this mountain, 'Get up and throw yourself into the sea,' with no hesitation in his heart but believing that what he says will happen, it will be done for him."

• • •**Q**   *And which New Testament text do you feel is most relevant for today's Christian?*

• • •**A**   I think the same texts that mean so much to me are relevant to others: the importance of a closeness with Jesus, to bear fruit for him, and the importance of having great faith. I also like passages that speak about living in praise and thanksgiving (1 Thess 5:16-18, for example)...those are like an antidote to too much introspection, worry and anxiety.

• • •**Q**   *Can you share any special personal experiences when Jesus has really touched your life?*

• • •**A**   One of the most touching experiences I've had was at Christmas Midnight Mass, in the first year of my theological studies. During that Mass I experienced a recurrent awareness that I had not chosen Christ, but that he had, in fact, chosen me. It was an extraordinarily consoling experience and it stands out in my memory. My other experiences have been less dramatic, but just as real—they involved the touch or embrace of God in prayer. That awareness of his presence and love, experienced from time to time in prayer, is very consoling.

• • •**Q** *Father, what's it like to attend very large gatherings and see so many people joined together in the Lord's name?*

• • •**A** Often at very large gatherings, especially at Charismatic conferences when the whole group sings in tongues, it's like a crescendo of praise. It really puts me in touch with the great mystery of God. I'm one who loves the liturgy in the vernacular, and I don't want to go back to the Latin, but I think that we may have lost something of the mystery of God in our current Eucharistic liturgies.

• • •**Q** *How do you feel when you know that the Lord has touched someone through your words?*

• • •**A** When I feel that people have been touched by something I say, I am both joy-filled and humbled...and I thank God for using me in my weakness.

Born in Providence, Rhode Island, in 1930, and ordained a priest in 1957, Fr. Ralph DiOrio, internationally renowned for his healing ministry, continues to be "a channel of God's incredible love."

RALPH DIORIO

• • •**Q** *Father, has your healing ministry changed your relationship with Jesus?*

• • •**A** I don't think so. I've not really found a decisive or definite change. The Christ I was preaching before I began this ministry is the same Christ I'm preaching today. On the other hand, I've found myself to be more free and more composed in the presence of the Lord who I walk with as a friend in my heart. And I know who I am; I'm neither living in the past, nor do I concern myself about the future. Rather, I always try to live in the present and make the best I can of it. And that reality, remaining in the present, is what I think has brought me into a life of continuous loyalty to the Master.

• • •**Q** *You distribute a holy card of Jesus which incorporates into his figure people of all different nationalities. Is that your image of Jesus?*

• • •**A** The picture is very indicative of me. It objectively portrays my spirit—in union with God and in union with all people. I've always felt that the cross of Jesus was for all of humanity, and I've never appreciated the many denominational differentiations. I think that's something the Lord put in me to prepare me for the work I now do.

• • •**Q**   *Father, in your ministry, you see so many people facing tremendous trials—of illness, of poverty—how do you handle it all?*

• • •**A**   The greatest struggle in my life is never to doubt God. Even though I may slip, get bruised, or make mistakes, that's all part of growth. And the sorrows that I see, the sorrows of my own life, I think that's God sculpturing us through the days of our lives. He helps us to drop the pretenses; he unmasks us—the false person—and the result is humility. You know, at the cross nobody stands tall.

• • •**Q**   *When you pray, do you picture Christ on the cross?*

• • •**A**   The Christ of my imagination is really the Christ I try to present to the public. I see Christ preaching love. I see Jesus, prior to the crucifixion, walking about as a happy troubadour, a man who's looking for the circle of love to be enriched with his arms. I see a manly, pleasant, affable, approachable person—a Christ who listens with a third ear, sees with a third eye, who is always alert, awake, ministering here and now. And I see the Christ willing to go to the cross.

• • •**Q**   *What is your favorite Scriptural passage? Which one speaks especially to you?*

• • •**A**   Because of the spiritual, emotional and psychological sorrows in my life, my mother's life, my family's life, I'm always drawn to the passion...the world is in such sorrow. But Christ left the tomb of death empty, and so I want to bring a rainbow of hope from Jesus. And I think the rainbow of hope encourages people to keep launching their own vessels into deeper waters.

• • •Q   *So, would you say the passion narratives are your favorite texts?*

• • •A   Really, my favorite Scriptural texts are those of the passion of Jesus as found in the Evangelists and also in St. Paul. I am especially fond of Ephesians 1:10, which says [in the Latin translation] *"Instaurare omnia in Christo"* ("To restore all things in Christ")—because that's how I see my mission as a priest, with the specific responsibilities flowing from the particular gift which the Lord has given to me. It's my duty to help restore all things in Christ.

• • •Q   *Father, how would you describe your personal relationship to Jesus Christ in the daily effort of trying to restore all things in him?*

• • •A   The power of faith in God is my relationship to the Lord...and sometimes it's difficult. I find that my relationship is a voyage of discovery into ever deeper walks of faith.

• • •Q   *Do you remember when this awareness of walking with the Lord became real for you?*

• • •A   Well, my mother was a very religious woman and she taught me all my first prayers. I guess though that my first conscious memory of Jesus goes back to when I was six. As my father was putting up a crucifix it dropped and broke, and I felt bad that the corpus of Christ had broken. I tried to repair it. A further awareness of Christ on the cross came through the influence of the Pallotine Sisters. As we would leave [the nursery] at night we'd all go to Mother Assunta, and she'd bless us and show us her cross, and we had to kiss it...always the cross.

• • •Q   *So you really grew up in a very religious atmosphere, didn't you?*

• • •**A**   Yes. I can remember one Good Friday when my grandfather took me to visit the statue of the dead Christ, laid out beautifully in the lower church of Saint Bartholomew in Providence, Rhode Island. The altar was decorated splendidly, with the body of Christ resting in the tomb. I was so impressed...I can still see it even now. And looking at the statue of the dead Christ, I asked my grandfather, "Who did that?"

• • •**Q**   *If Jesus came back to earth today, is that the question you would ask him?*

• • •**A**   I think my question would be: Is it you? Is it really you?

• • •**Q**   *Father, I know that you have seen many miracles. Are there one or two that stand out in your mind, ones in which you felt that Jesus especially touched you?*

• • •**A**   Let me say that I don't count healings. The day that I try to do that, or ask which miracle was more extraordinary, then I've lost the power of healing. I would not feel I had the gifts of the Lord if I started to evaluate which are the "better" ones. You know, during the healing services I feel like a little boy running around with my toy, saying to the Lord, "We've got four hours here, Lord, let's play our game today." And he's using me as I'm touching this person, touching that one. Moreover, every healing, whether it's big or small, is very subjective. What is small to me is great to someone else. What I can say is, that in all these fifteen years of my healing ministry, I can't picture anything great, in the tangible way, because I look for answers and affirmation from God and not from anyone else. When I was in India, I looked out at this vast crowd of people listening to the bishop as he preached, and waiting for me to speak—they were sitting everywhere, up in the trees, on the rooftops, 135,000 or 200,000 people—and the word of the Lord came to me, "Ralph, my son, my gift to you is the gift of my people." And I think that is the miracle that has touched me to tears. When I get discouraged or I'm criticized, it doesn't really matter. I have Christ's words: "Ralph, my son, I give to you the gift of my people."

• • •Q   *How do you describe your ministry to people? Do you approach them, or allow them to approach you, for the purpose of healing?*

• • •A   I tell people: you come to me because you don't want sickness and disease and because you're looking for healing. I will respect, with compassion, your sickness and disease, and do whatever I can in prayer. However, my love for Christ and you goes deeper than compassion; I have the responsibility to take you to Christ. And that's evangelization!

• • •Q   *So, you are known as a healer, but you see yourself as an evangelizer first?*

• • •A   Yes, without evangelization I would be a phony and a farce!

• • •Q   *Would you say that your work of evangelization and healing has been successful?*

• • •A   Oh, yes, and for millions and millions of people. And the real healings, the real blessings are the spiritual. I'll tell you a story: At one of the services I was walking down the center aisle blessing people with holy water, and near the back of the church was a little old crippled woman. I would have given five years of my life for her to be healed.... I think she saw the sorrow on my face because she said, "Fr. Ralph, don't look so sad, tonight I was healed." And because I'm a priest I knew that she would add, "Tonight, after forty-four years, I have found my God again."

• • •**Q**   *And is that what it's really all about?*

• • •**A**   Yes, that's it! At my ordination I asked for three gifts and two of them have already come to me. The first was that I would always appreciate my daily Mass and love the Eucharist with devotion all my life. The second was that God would give me the grace to preach, and touch souls, and I've received those. The third grace I asked for was martyrdom of blood—to die as a martyr at the altar—that hasn't come yet.

• • •**Q**   *Maybe it will come in a form you don't expect?*

• • •**A**   Yes, I know it will.

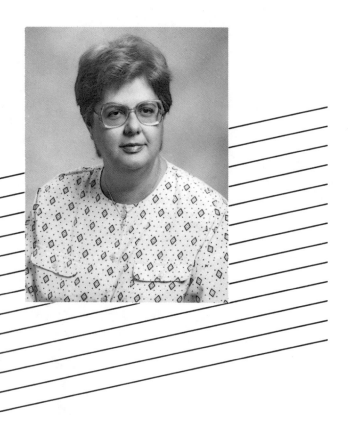

Deeply concerned with fostering the role of the laity in the Church, Adele Gonzalez currently serves as associate director for the Office of Lay Ministry in the Archdiocese of Miami. In dioceses across the country, Adele is a frequent lecturer on spirituality and the role of the laity in the Church today.

ADELE GONZALEZ

• • •**Q** *Adele, how did you got involved with lay ministry and spiritual direction?*

• • •**A** Well, a few years ago people began asking me for help in their spiritual life. I felt that I needed some training in order to properly respond so I enrolled in the spiritual direction program at the Shalem Institute in Washington, DC. Since then, people have continued to ask my help with spiritual direction. My main concern now in the Office of Lay Ministry is with formation, and over the last three years I've been invited to several dioceses to give talks and lectures to various groups.

• • •**Q** *And what sort of message do you seek to communicate through those talks?*

• • •**A** Of course, the topics vary depending on the group and what they've asked me to speak about. But, whatever the topic, I want to convey to my listeners the goodness of God and the unconditional love of God...because I find that most people either have not experienced it or don't believe in it.

• • •**Q** *Adele, what were some times when you especially felt that unconditional love in your life?*

• • •**A**   Perhaps the first and most significant time was when my father died. I was thirteen and I didn't have a strong religious background, so when he died my question was, "Well, where is he? What happens now?" And nobody seemed to have an answer that would satisfy me. My father was a Mason who believed in God, and for some reason had a tremendous love for Mary, but other than that, in terms of church attendance, etc., he was not an active Catholic. So I thought: "Oh my God, he's in hell." During that time of doubt and confusion, a friend invited me to go on a weekend retreat for teenagers, and during the retreat I went to confession. I told the priest that my father was in hell and that it was my fault because I had not been a good Catholic. At that time I would usually have been given ten Hail Mary's as a penance and sent on my way. Instead the priest questioned me and then invited me to speak with him outside the confessional.

• • •**Q**   *Was that the beginning of your conversion?*

• • •**A**   Yes, that was the beginning of two years of weekly meetings, during which he gave me spiritual direction and instruction. One of the first things Father asked me was if I knew God. I said that, really, I didn't. Then he asked, "Adele, if you were God and your father came now in front of you, what would you do?" I answered that I would give him a big hug and welcome him into my kingdom. And the priest said, "Well, why do you think you're better than God? Obviously, you don't yet know God's goodness." And that was a moment of grace for me.

• • •**Q**   *Adele, you seem very convinced of that love today! When you pray, how do you visualize Jesus? Who is the person of Jesus for you?*

•••**A**   I really don't have an image of Jesus—nor have I ever felt a need to picture the human Jesus. But I do have an experience (not an image) of what he probably looked like. You see, what turned me on originally—as a teenager—to the whole Christian message came out of a tremendous commitment to the Gospel message. It did not come from an encounter with the historical Jesus. The power of the Gospel message itself was so alive, so real to me that the looks of the human person who had given the message were not that important.

•••**Q**   *So often when I've gone into an Hispanic home, I've seen these giant, beautiful pictures of Jesus—a devotional portrayal of a very warm and loving Jesus. How is it that your experience seems so different?*

•••**A**   I remember being turned off by those pictures because they did not relate to what I was hearing in the Gospel message. I was hearing a message of commitment to the poor, of giving oneself totally—a very radical message that didn't go with the curly hair and the blue eyes and the clean white robe. Neither did it seem to go with our dramatic Holy Week portrayal of Christ's passion. It was all on the emotional level, and I didn't see people changing their lives because of it. It didn't impress me.

•••**Q**   *Adele, do you think that growing up in Cuba during the 1950's had an impact on your spiritual development?*

•••**A**   Yes. Born as I was in 1945, and very much aware of the whole Fidel Castro thing—especially when revolution was so much in the air among the youth—I clung to the Gospel message and not to the historical man behind that message who had suffered and died on the cross...because he was a symbol of defeat. You see, the historical man who had died didn't mean anything because there were other people who had died for me. The resurrection didn't mean anything because it couldn't be historically proven. But because I did not find the message of the Gospel—the message of God's unconditional love—in any of the marches or any of the speeches, I remained attracted to that message. The message really came before the person.

• • •**Q**   *You've been talking about the message of the Gospel, which of the Gospel texts do you find most challenging?*

• • •**A**   There are several which challenge me. I think of the whole turning upside down of things as found in the Beatitudes, and the call to love of enemies, the old law versus the new law—and our calling to be light and salt. And in terms of mission, I think of everything that has to do with "go." I often say that the most important words in the New Testament are "come" and "go." It's like, come and see, and go and tell. That is the whole freedom of the Christian, to come and see, and then go tell what you have seen.

• • •**Q**   *And are there particular texts which give you comfort in your ministry?*

• • •**A**   Well, all the parables which speak of God's unconditional love. And the raising of Lazarus where we read that Jesus cried—knowing that Jesus showed emotions, that he shared his own pain and shared in the pain of that family—that is very comforting. And then, in the Gospel of John, Jesus prays, "I have come that they may have life and life to the fullest" (cf Jn 10:10), and, "This is eternal life, that they may know you, the only true God, and Jesus Christ..." (cf Jn 17:3). It's good for me to know that *life* is to know God in a very deep way, and to know Jesus Christ.

• • •**Q**   *And who is Jesus for you today? Is he teacher, healer, friend, Lord?*

• • •**A**   Well, as a young adult I was influenced by the writings of Teilhard de Chardin, so I related to Christ as the Omega, the beginning and the end, and that kind of thing. I did not relate to the historical Jesus until I came to know Francis of Assisi. I met Jesus through Francis. He was so different from me—simple, sincere, extraverted.... But I also found that I couldn't put my hands on him because he was always moving me away from himself and back to the Gospel. Francis was so Jesus-centered that I could not meet Francis without finding out who Jesus was. Francis brought me to Jesus the poor man, the simple person. And so, today I experience Jesus as someone who is journeying with me.

• • •**Q**   *How do you nurture and express that relationship with Jesus?*

• • •**A**   Prayer. That's number one. And it's probably number two and three and four. My natural tendency is towards a silent contemplative prayer, whether it be centering prayer or any other technique, it doesn't really matter. I read Scripture a lot and I like to pray with the Psalms...but mostly I would say it's in silence that I really encounter God.

Born in New York City, Dolores Bernadette Grier was reared in Harlem as a Baptist and converted to the Roman Catholic faith in her teens. Foundress of the Association of Black Catholics Against Abortion, she obtained a Master's degree in Social Service from the University of Fordham and has been awarded an Honorary Doctorate in Human Letters from Iona College, New York, as well as an Honorary Doctorate in Law from St. John's University in New York. In 1985, Dolores Bernadette Grier was appointed by John Cardinal O'Connor as the first lay person to hold the position of vice-chancellor in the Archdiocese of New York.

DOLORES BERNADETTE GRIER

• • •Q *Dr. Grier, as the first woman, and the first Black American, to be a vice-chancellor in the Archdiocese of New York, what have some of your duties been these last seven years?*

• • •A Well, as a vice-chancellor for Community Relations, I really am an ambassador from the Cardinal to the people of the Archdiocese and the community-at-large, and I am also an ambassador from the community back to the Cardinal. I get a lot of invitations to speak and share my life and experiences—recently I was asked to speak on "the joy of being a Catholic woman." I also speak on being Roman Catholic and proud, pro-life, evangelizing the family...I am overwhelmed with requests, but I enjoy my work very much.

• • •Q *I know that you frequently speak about devotion to Mary and the Rosary Crusade. Why is that? Why emphasize the Rosary?*

• • •A Oh! If the women of today would use our Blessed Lady as their role model, what loving and holy families we would have. Women would respect themselves in speech, dress and person—and would be respected in turn. Loving, caring and serving—these

53

virtues which are natural to women—would enhance the family unit of husband, wife and children. I always carry extra rosaries with me, should the occasion arise that I can share it with someone and encourage devotion to our Blessed Mother.

• • •**Q**   *I know you travel a good deal and have a heavy schedule, but when you stop the activity and close your eyes and speak to Jesus, can you describe how he looks?*

• • •**A**   I see Jesus with outstretched arms, inviting me to "Come..., all you who are burdened and I will give you rest" (cf Mt 11:28). Being an historian of Black American culture, I am often reminded of one of the spirituals sung by the slaves in this country: "Leaning on the Everlasting Arms." In all that the slaves endured—whippings, rapes, lynchings, burnings—their refuge was the "everlasting arms of Jesus Christ!"

• • •**Q**   *So that is your image, Jesus with outstretched arms?*

• • •**A**   Yes, the outstretched arms of Jesus Christ, inviting all who are in the state of confusion, concern, chaos, crises—all who are trying to conquer sin in this satanistic society—to come to him and find love and peace of mind.

• • •**Q**   *And how would you describe Jesus' temperament? What part of his personality most appeals to you?*

• • •**A**   The way Jesus always sought solace from God, his Father, appeals to me. Jesus would take leave of the apostles and the crowds and go off alone in prayer. Today many of us do not take time to talk with God, our Father. We are too busy with the things of the world. Although Jesus was busy—being a role model and teacher for the apostles, preaching the Word of

God, healing and curing people, consoling the bereaved, contending with the Pharisees and with Martha—Jesus found time, made time to pray to God. We, too, need God. We cannot survive Satan—who is alive and seeking whom he may devour—without going to God, our Father, in prayer.

• • •**Q** *When you pray, which of the Gospel texts do you find most comforting, most challenging?*

• • •**A** For me, I find the passages, "If you love me, keep my commandments..." (cf Jn 14:15), and, "If you want to follow me...take up your cross" (cf Mk 8:34), to be the most challenging texts.

• • •**Q** *That certainly is a challenge!*

• • •**A** Yes indeed! And some days the cross is heavier than others. The telephone rings and someone has a crisis. You step on the elevator and are greeted by a neighbor with "good morning," and the greeting is followed by a request for help with a problem. The legislator smiles, thanks you for your visit, assures you he is in accord, then votes against the bill. The mail at home or in the office brings comments and criticism from angry Catholics who disagree with some aspect of Church teachings. You wonder, why me? Why should I care? Why should I have to defend the Roman Catholic faith to Roman Catholics? Then you remember the words of Jesus Christ, "If you want to follow me, take up your cross and come follow me." What a challenge!

• • •**Q** *And the most comforting Gospel passage?*

• • •**A** "Come to me, all you who are burdened and I will give you rest." And, "Lo, I am always with you..." (cf Mt 28:20). It is comforting to know that Jesus is always there.

• • •**Q** *When you think of Jesus' different titles—teacher, rescuer, healer, friend, Lord—which do you identify with?*

• • •**A** Savior! Jesus Christ, Savior of my soul. I believe that Jesus would have suffered and died on the cross just for me alone. Yes, Jesus is all of the titles you mention, but to me he is my Savior who gave his life for me on the cross. As we sing in the Negro Spiritual, "I'm So Glad Jesus Lifted Me!" His death and resurrection lifted me from sin. Alleluia! Another title I'd say is friend. Jesus is indeed my friend. Another Negro Spiritual sums it up: "What a Friend I have in Jesus." What a friend we have in Jesus. "All our sins and griefs to bear. What a privilege to carry everything to him in prayer. Are we weak and heavy laden, cumbered with a load of care, Precious Savior, still our refuge, take it to the Lord in prayer. In his arms he will shield you, and you will find solace there."

I also identify with Jesus as teacher. Jesus was a teacher and role model for the apostles. Through the Scriptures, he is teacher and role model for us today. And Jesus is leader, a loving shepherd who leads his flock to God the Father. Regretfully, many call themselves Christians but do not follow Jesus. They drift from his flock. They would not be lost if they would only return to the Savior!

• • •**Q** *And how do you nurture and deepen your own love relationship with Jesus?*

• • •**A** Through the Sacraments, especially the Eucharist. The Body of Jesus sustains me in all situations. I have a special devotion to Jesus in the Blessed Sacrament—I could sit with him for hours. When I leave his Presence, I am revived, renewed, restored and better prepared for this satanistic society. Following daily Mass, I spend at least a half hour in the presence of

Jesus in the Most Blessed Sacrament. I look forward to the day when Jesus in the Blessed Sacrament is once more at the center of the altar in every Roman Catholic Church. Perhaps then many Catholics will bring him back to the center of their lives. Joy filled my heart when his Eminence, John Cardinal O'Connor, established, for the first time in the history of Saint Patrick's Cathedral, the First Friday Nocturnal Devotions. And at least twice a year I go on retreat to strengthen my personal relationship with Jesus. In addition, I pray the Rosary and have great devotion to our Blessed Mother.

• • •**Q**   *Dr. Grier, if Jesus came back to earth today what question would you like to ask him? If he spoke on prime time television, what would you hope that he would speak about?*

• • •**A**   If Jesus Christ returned to earth I certainly would not ask him anything—I would stand in awe of his presence and kneel in reverence, filled with joy that my Savior was here with me. Were he to speak publicly, I hope he would address the topic of love: the love of God, our Father, the love of ourselves, and the love of our neighbor as ourselves. There is too much hatred in the world today and I believe it stems from a lack of love for God, self and others. If we say we love God, then we must love his creation; we are God's creation, made in his image and to his likeness. When we sincerely believe this then we will love ourselves and our neighbor.

A founding member of the Franciscan Friars of the Renewal—a fraternity in the Capuchin tradition—Fr. Benedict Joseph Groeschel, CFR, is a psychologist, professor, retreat director, director of the New York Archdiocesan Office for Spiritual Development, and promoter of the cause for the beatification of Terence Cardinal Cooke.

BENEDICT JOSEPH GROESCHEL, CFR

• • •**Q** *Let's start with your perception of Jesus—your own personal images as a friar-priest and psychologist.*

• • •**A** I don't have a visual image in my mind of what our Lord looked like, but the paintings of Christ which impress me the most are by Fra Angelico. Being something of a fourteenth-century person myself, I am most at home with those images. When I was in the seminary I had a difficult time and, consequently, for several years the only books I read (other than required reading for school) were different lives of Christ written by Scriptural theologians of the day: Pratt, Ricciotti, and others. I read all of the great Christological sermons: St. Augustine and the other early fathers of the Church. Whatever fiction I read dealt with Christ-figures, for example, the works of Dostoevsky and Leon Bloy.

• • •**Q** *So, from your early seminary days you had a strong attraction to Christ—was there any one aspect of Christ's life that attracted you?*

• • •**A** I find the passion and death of Christ to be central to my thinking. However, for me Christ has several meanings. First of all, he was the Word of God in whom all things are made. In common with most

Franciscans, I have a sense of the beauty of the material world and the presence of Christ in the forests, the fields and the stars. Secondly, I experience the presence of Christ in the suffering, the poor, the dying, the sinner. Christ is hidden there. When I go to the foreign missions I also go to the pagan temples to pray. Why? Because Christ is hidden even there....

• • •**Q**   *Could you say then that Christ is really always present to you?*

• • •**A**   Christ is the most real person in my life. There has been no question about that ever since I was nineteen or twenty years old. That is why I take a very dim view of the present day crypto-arians who seem to be belittling the divinity of Christ. I think when you turn Christ into something less than the Incarnate Word, God from God, Light from Light, true God from true God, then you miss the mystery of Christ. Arius was a very intelligent priest, who, in my opinion, accidently fell into a kind of baptized paganism because he turned Christ into a demigod, that is, half a god, half a man, like a centaur. Today, all who leave out the mysterious seem to fall into crypto-arianism.

• • •**Q**   *You seem to have a great sense of the mystery of God....*

• • •**A**   For me the word you *must* use with Christ is mysterious. I become very annoyed when people tell me what Christ knew and what he didn't know. They present a Christ who didn't know who and what he was. I become infuriated, because these speculations are based on both an ignorance of child psychology and a deliberate attempt to side step the teachings of the early ecumenical councils—and even of the Scriptures themselves.

• • •**Q** *What about his personality? I know that nobody likes to label it. But of all the personality types....*

• • •**A** According to Professor Gordon Allport, the great expert on this subject, a personality is a moving, dynamic configuration of strengths, weaknesses and potentials. Most psychologists see defense mechanisms as a very significant part of personality functioning— most of us would be very different people from who we are without our defense mechanisms. In fact, Christ did not have defense mechanisms. They are distortions of reality, and that is what Christ didn't have. He simply did not experience the effects of original sin. So, in the sense that we use the word personality, I don't think Christ had one. He is simply a person. We are persons who relate to reality through personality. Christ is simply a divine person, and this certainly makes it clear that he would not have a number of the elements of human personality that are effects of original sin.

• • •**Q** *Then what do you think it would have been like to actually meet Jesus?*

• • •**A** It is difficult for me to imagine what my initial reaction would be to Christ, except to say that I would be frightened. Why? Because here's somebody who knows what I am thinking. He knows everything about me—and can tell me to do something and I can't even argue with him. It is rather intimidating to think of meeting Christ. Now, what was he like? Obviously he was extraordinarily compassionate, as we see in his actions towards several people who were in a great deal of trouble: the woman taken in adultery, the woman at the well. He was also a very devout, observant, prayer-ful Jew, who went through all of the rituals, but appar-ently not in the driven way that many religious people do because he was able to put these in perspective. He was also confrontational. When it came to the things of God there was absolutely no area of compromise. This quality is amazingly united to a person who was very compassionate. Christ was also very Jewish. I think we miss some of the best lines in the New Testament because we fail to realize that they were written in the Jewish community. We lose some of the ironic humor of Christ. We make his picture, the New Testament, so terribly solemn that we lose the tang of the whole thing. Jesus was one of those very vital, tangy people. He was anything but the kind of sickly looking figure that we see in our stained glass windows. He was not insipid.

• • •Q   *What is your favorite Gospel quotation? What setting makes you say, "Now, that's the Jesus I like. That's an event at which I wish I'd been present"?*

• • •A   It would be the fourteenth to the seventeenth chapter of the Gospel of St. John. Scholars argue about whether these are actually the words of our Lord or the spiritual teaching of the very early Church. I believe that substantively he said these things. So my favorite quotation is, "If anyone would open to me, my Father and I will come to him and make our home with him" (cf Jn 14:23). Also, "If you keep my word you shall be my disciples. You shall know the truth and the truth will make you free" (cf Jn 8:31-32). These are rather awesome, inspiring words. I suppose they have to be balanced with the very opposite quotation where Christ warns Peter that Satan will sift him as wheat, but that he will return and confirm his brethren. So these are very contrasting quotations and it is important to remember that right after the beautiful words at the Last Supper, the disciples did, in fact, betray Jesus Christ.

• • •Q   *The words from your favorite quote, "The Father*

and I will dwell with him," what kind of Jesus said that? How do you understand being one with Christ?

• • •A   These are the most mystical words that Jesus spoke; they are also terribly intimate. And, if I knew the answer to that question I would be dead! This is the transcendent union with God that we are called to, the ultimate meaning of the whole spiritual life and the Christian life—it is absolutely mysterious. We come to it only after this life.

• • •Q   *Can we get there through our good works?*

• • •A   No! We get there absolutely through the grace of Christ. You and I can't merit it in any way at all. However, we must cooperate by good works done in response to living faith. This is the teaching of the Catholic tradition. Don't be surprised by my total dependency on Christ. Remember, I'm a disciple of St. Augustine, who said to Christ: "You are the physician and I am the sick man. Make me well!"

• • •Q   *Father, can you point to any particular time when you consciously experienced Jesus acting in your life?*

• • •A   I can say that I was seven years old when Jesus Christ delivered me from evil—and all of my life I have been aware of the problem of evil. I had an experience with a lady who I thought was a witch and who frightened the life out of me. And that very day while kneeling in front of the statue of the Blessed Virgin Mary I realized that I was supposed to be a priest.

A second experience came when I was twelve. Its basis was a marvelous poem by Longfellow called "The Legend Beautiful," from *Tales of a Wayside Inn*. This poem tells of a monk who was in charge of taking care of the poor people. One day he was praying and had a vision of Christ. The bell rang, summoning him to feed the poor at the door of the monastery. Should he go to the poor or stay with the vision of Christ? He doesn't know what to do. A voice within him says, "Do thy duty, that is best! Leave unto the Lord the rest!" The monk goes and leaves the vision and takes care of the poor. As he is working with them he again hears the voice from within, "Whatsoever thing thou doest unto the least of mine and lowest, thou doest unto Me."

The poem then continues with this powerful passage: "Unto Me! but had the Vision Come to him in beggar's clothing, Come a mendicant imploring, Would he then have knelt adoring, Or have listened with derision, And have turned away with loathing? Thus his conscience put the question, Full of troublesome suggestion, As at length, with hurried pace, Towards his cell he turned his face, And beheld the convent bright With a supernatural light, Like a luminous cloud expanding Over floor and wall and ceiling." He rushes back to his room after he feeds the poor, and the vision was still there. The Lord tells him, "Hadst thou stayed, I must have fled!"

• • •Q   *You read that when you were twelve?*

• • •A   I memorized it when I was twelve. It is such an important part of my life that if I have an opportunity to plan for my funeral, I'm going to have that poem distributed at it. It really is the essence of what I've been trying to do in the course of my life.

• • •Q   *How do you nurture your relationship with Christ? And how do you express that relationship?*

• • •A   First of all, by the daily celebration of Eucharist. Then, our community requires a daily Eucharistic Holy Hour as part of our rule of life. I also try to express my relationship to Christ in the service of the poor. Just about a month ago one of the men in the shelter came in with a very bad abscess in his arm. He had been stung by a bee and now had an infection. It was too late at night to send him to the emergency room, but since I had been an infirmarian I knew how to drain it. The abscess was very large and smelled; it took an hour to drain. And I must say that the clearest experience of the suffering of Christ that I have had in years I had in caring for that poor man. As the poem by Longfellow says: "At the gate the poor were waiting, Looking through the iron grating, With that terror in the eye That is only seen in those Who amid their wants and woes Hear the sound of doors that close, And of feet that pass them by Grown familiar with disfavor, Grown familiar with the savor Of the bread by which men die."

• • •**Q** *Father, can you share any other moments when Jesus' presence was very strong in your life?*

• • •**A** I think the most moving experience was in the Atlantic Avenue Jail (a huge jail in New York, mainly for young men). In those days I was much thinner and I had a red beard. One day I was waiting for the inmates to be put back in their cells so that I could visit. As I waited, an officer ran in and asked if I'd go upstairs—a boy had just hung himself. I went to the end of the cell block and saw some inmates and the prison doctor standing near a young Hispanic man lying on the floor. They had torn off his shirt and were giving him artificial respiration. He had hung himself, but the belt had broken. I asked what the charge was against him and was told that he was a drug addict and that he had been an accomplice in a robbery where a man was killed. The prison doctor said to me, "He's OK, Father. He just knocked the air out of his lungs." But I thought, how can he be OK? The man had just attempted suicide! So as the inmates and doctor moved away, I knelt down on the floor beside him, holding his head in my hands. In a while he opened his eyes and smiled at me. It was such a beautiful smile, but I sensed something was wrong. There was something that didn't fit. And then I realized that this man thought he was dead! After hanging himself, he had opened his eyes and there's a man in a robe (I was dressed in my habit), with a red beard, looking at him. He thought I was Someone else. I moved my head so he could see the cell block and he started to cry. He cried for half an hour. I just sat there on the floor crying with him. Oddly enough, this boy's name was Salvatore. I've never forgotten that incident, although it happened twenty-five years ago. We use the phrase "seeing Christ" in people. It's an intellectual idea and a very good one, and we do the best we can with it. But sometimes an experience of seeing Christ in other people hits us right in the face; and often we don't respond very well. We look and say: Christ couldn't possibly be speaking to me through this prostitute, that person with AIDS.... And yet, in Matthew, chapter 25, we are told that he is hiding there. You see, Christ is not that person; but in the particular situation his presence is there. The young man on the prison floor was a poor kid who was a drug addict and got involved in a felony murder. Christ isn't that man, but he's really there in him in the situation. It's regrettable that we don't respond better to that Presence.

*A Philadelphia homemaker, author
and lecturer, Molly Kelly centers
her apostolic efforts on presenting
Christ's message of chastity and
respect for the human person.
Widowed in 1975, she has raised
eight children and has still found
time to speak to thousands of
teenagers throughout the United
States and Canada, inviting them to
choose chastity as a way to health
and happiness.*

MOLLY KELLY

• • •Q *Molly, would you begin by telling me some of the things that occupy your twenty-four hour day? A day which, I think, you stretch to forty-eight hours?*

• • •A Well, first is my family; they're the most important people in my life. And since my children are grown and demand less attention now, I spend a lot of time speaking to young people on the issues of abortion and respect for life, especially on chastity, which I see as the solution to abortion. I speak to about fifty thousand young people each year, telling them that saved sex, s-a-v-e-d, is the alternative to safe sex.

• • •Q *I know that you spoke at a priests' retreat held in the Vatican, several thousand priests were there, weren't there?*

• • •A Yes. There were six thousand priests from all over the world, many of them from third world countries. It was an absolutely amazing event. I came home with a renewed reverence and love for the priesthood.

• • •Q *Why were you asked to speak to the priests on the topic of chastity?*

• • •A I was not really assigned that topic. But I chose to speak about the need for priests to talk about chastity from the pulpit, on retreats, and in the classrooms. I reminded priests that they too are sexual persons, and asked them to tell our young people that sexuality is a gift. I asked them to bring people back to the Sacrament of Reconciliation, to talk about it, to talk about the abortion issue.... I told them that when they speak about abortion they should not be afraid that a women in the congregation might be hurt by their words. I stressed that women might, in fact, be healed through their words. And the response from those six thousand priests was a standing ovation.

• • •**Q**   *Molly, when you pray, how do you see Jesus? What is your image of him?*

• • •**A**   Well, I'm somebody who has to concretize things. So I picture Jesus as a young man, early thirties. I see him as handsome with longish hair, the kind of hair that I'd probably give my boys a hard time about...but on Jesus it looks good. I see him as rugged but gentle. But, what really strikes me most when I'm praying are his eyes—piercing, bright, happy, but with a tinge of sadness. I see his eyes as inquisitive, asking me what went on today; asking me if I want to talk about it. I also see his eyes as very affirming in that I know he has all the answers for me. When I picture him looking at me I see him looking through me; he can see my innermost feelings. Jesus talks to me, through his eyes, without even saying a word.

Another picture that frequently comes to me is Jesus on the cross. I love the crucifix used by Pope John Paul II, the figure of the broken Christ. It's powerful because his arms are out of the sockets, hanging, nothing's holding them, his knees are spread apart, his head is drooping.... That crucifix gives me a real sense of the agony of the cross, which makes me all the more aware of the gift of the cross.

• • •**Q**   *Do you ever imagine what kind of character or temperament Jesus had? What do you think he was like?*

• • •**A**   What's neatest about Jesus is that he became man; he allows us to really get to know him. He was like us in everything but sin. He felt cold, worked, learned carpentry, walked, ran, wept openly, laughed heartily just as we do. When I'm thinking of Jesus and his character, the word "peaceful" always comes to me. Even when he was upset, he was so full of peace. As for virtue and temperament, obviously Jesus is everything, all virtue. However, I would single out honesty. I love Jesus' honesty. And his forgiveness is also something that moves me.

• • •**Q**   *Molly, when you read through the New Testament which words of Jesus are most comforting for you?*

• • •**A**   Jesus' words from the cross to the good thief: "This day you'll be with me in paradise" (cf Lk 23:43). That's powerful and comforting for me. I also find "Come to me, all you who are heavily burdened..." very comforting (cf Mt 11:28-29). You know, a mother who has eight children can be heavily burdened. And in all our burdens, Jesus says, "Come to me and I will give you rest." Another comforting text is "My Father has prepared a mansion for you" (cf Jn 14:2). I live in a big house, and I think it would be neat to live in a big house up there that I don't have to clean.

• • •**Q**   *Only a mother of eight would think of that one! Which words of Jesus do you find most challenging?*

• • •**A**   What is challenging to me, and scary, is Matthew's account of Judgment Day (cf Mt 25). In fact, it's frightening because we're really told what's going to happen. And I think it's a terrifying account of the last days and God's justice and judgment and how alone we'll be before the Lord. The challenge is to be ever watchful. We don't know the day, or the moment—so Christ gave us the parable of the wise and foolish virgins.... What all this says to me is that I should think of each day, not necessarily as my last, but that it could be my last. And therefore any way I can obtain grace— through the Sacraments or visits to the Blessed Sacrament—helps me to get ready. And through my ministry I want to help others get ready. I want the Jesus in me to touch and meet the Jesus in others. I want people to be able to see the Jesus in me. And I want to tap into the Jesus in other people.

• • •**Q** *And what name or title do you use in prayer with Jesus?*

• • •**A** I like to think of and call him, "Teacher." Because that's what I do and that's what he did. I try to be like Jesus, the teacher, and call on him before every talk, asking him to speak through me. I also think of Jesus as Savior. Jesus as teacher in my work—Jesus as Savior in my own personal life, in that he died on the cross for me. I also like the title of companion. I often travel alone and Jesus is my companion on trips.

• • •**Q** *Molly, how would you describe your own personal relationship with Jesus?*

• • •**A** I describe my personal relationship with Jesus as something that is ongoing, constant. When I return home from a trip I have to catch up with my kids, and I have to do exactly the same with Jesus. And that's done through prayer, reception of the Sacraments, etc. So, I have an ongoing relationship that has to be worked at on my part.

• • •**Q** *It's obvious that you are very much at home and comfortable in your relationship with Jesus, and that it's been* *in place for quite some time. Think back and tell us when this relationship really began....*

• • •A   Well, I grew up in a Catholic home and attended Catholic schools all my life. If you had asked me as a child if I loved Jesus I would have said yes. But I'm not so sure I knew what that meant. I'd have to say that my relationship with Jesus really began when I married Jim Kelly. He was a physician and, although I don't want to make him bigger in death than in life, he was a gentle and Christ-like man. Through his life, Jim made me more aware of Christ, and that awareness deepened when Jim died. I was left alone, and neither my children nor my friends could really comfort me. The only comfort I had was the belief that Jim was with God. When we married we made a pact that we were going to get to heaven—and he went on ahead of me. He's there, and I'm going to join him. The kids, too, are absolutely sure they're going to go—because they know that when I get there I'll badger God and bend his ear until I get them to heaven!

• • •Q   *Molly, the shock of early deaths can turn the survivors closer to God or push them far away from God. In your case, Jim's death seems to have brought you closer to God. Can you comment on that?*

• • •A   I feel that I was blessed in that I didn't experience bitterness or anger when Jim died. Of course, I wasn't happy about Jim's death—it was a freak accident while we were out sledding with the kids—but my overriding sense was of loss and loneliness. And that can be as painful as bitterness or anger. But that sense of aloneness ("You're alone...you'll never be anyone's priority as you were Jim's") brought me to a great awareness of both God's presence and Jim's—it was the grace of the Holy Spirit.

• • •**Q**   *Have there been other occasions in your life when Jesus touched you in a unique way?*

• • •**A**   I went to Medjugorje two years ago, and Jesus was so present to me through his mother! I'm a mother of six sons, and it makes perfect sense to me to go through a mother to get to her son. Going to Medju–gorje not only strengthened my relationship with Mary, but also with Jesus. I didn't go for signs, although many interesting things happened, but the really big thing that happened was the strengthening of my relationship with Jesus. Medjugorje is a little village; I felt as if I was in Nazareth, with Jesus and his family.

• • •**Q**   *If Jesus were to appear on prime time television, what would you like him to talk about?*

• • •**A**   Jesus on prime time TV...that would be amaz-ing! They'd shut him down in a minute because he's too controversial. Well, on prime time TV I would definitely want him to speak about abortion and chastity because you'd be amazed at the number of people who are convinced that the Bible does not take a stand on abor-tion. You'd be amazed at how many people know that the sixth commandment forbids adultery, but do not understand why premarital sex is wrong. So I'd like to hear him ask, "What are you telling our young people? What did you do to the gift of sexuality that I gave to you? Why are you soiling it? Why are you presenting it as simply a biological function?" I'd like to see Jesus on prime time TV and hear him put the fear of God in us—because he is God. And I'd love to hear him say, "Thou shalt not kill unborn children in the womb. The blood of unborn children on the hands of abortionists is abomi-nable. I will forgive you if you seek my pardon."

• • •**Q**   *Molly, how do you maintain such a dynamic relationship with Christ?*

• • •**A** I try to nurture it at daily Mass—I love the Eucharist and I spend time daily before the Blessed Sacrament. During that time I picture Jesus, focus my eyes on him, read Scripture.... And I think that Jesus is speaking through me. I think that one of the greatest gifts Jesus gave us, a gift which I only recently became aware of in such a tremendous way, is the Holy Spirit. At my Confirmation I understood something about the Holy Spirit, but I don't think I understood it as I do now. It's absolutely awesome, and the Holy Spirit helps me in my work.

• • •**Q** *How do you experience that help?*

• • •**A** I sometimes give six or seven talks a day, and I pray to the Holy Spirit for energy, for enthusiasm— because I only get one shot at the kids—and I've never, ever not been given the energy and enthusiasm needed to do God's work.

• • •**Q** *Molly, you really see your message of chastity as God's work, don't you?*

• • •**A** Yes, and I have the absolute conviction that Jesus is saying to me, "Molly, I told you that I'm with you, and that you are making a difference. Not you, Molly Kelly, but you, allowing me to speak through you, are making a difference." And I can see it, feel it, and I know the impact. Not because I'm so wonderful, but because I'm the tool that Jesus is using to make an impact. And that's exciting!

Raised in a devout family in the Reformed Church, Peter Kreeft entered the Roman Catholic Church as a young adult while attending Yale University. A renowned author and lecturer, he is currently a professor of philosophy at Boston College.

PETER KREEFT

• • •**Q** *Peter, when I compare certain Scripture scenes,
such as Jesus saying, "Consider the lilies of the field," with
others, such as Jesus throwing out the money changers, I get
two different pictures of Jesus. Do you ever experience
anything like that?*

• • •**A** Yes, but then they come together. That is, if
you read all the Gospels, you remember that the Jesus
who threw out the money changers is the same Jesus
who talked about the lilies of the fields. The picture of
Jesus that I have in my mind is not a sensorial image,
but more of a concept. And this is so because my picture is a conglomerate of all the things that Jesus said
and did in the Gospels. It's like what Sheldon Vanauken
called the "David Copperfield effect" in his book, *A
Severe Mercy*. He wrote that it was only after his wife
died that he really came to know her fully. Why? Because she was like a book, and death ended the book.
And after you've read all of *David Copperfield*, you can
say the word "David Copperfield" and mean the whole
of him. However, when you're in the middle of reading
it, and you say "David Copperfield," you mean only the
adolescent David, or the young David, or the David of a
particular section of the book. So with Christ: the Christ

of the Gospels is the Christ who on the one hand is incredibly tender and on the other hand is incredibly stern. In his tenderness you remember his sternness, and in his sternness you remember his tenderness.

• • •**Q** *So, how do you picture Jesus Christ?*

• • •**A** My imaginative picture of Christ really comes from the Gospels, so I don't have a picture of Christ in the sense of popular religious art—most post-renaissance religious art doesn't move me very much.... If I am to picture Christ in a concrete way, it will be more in the symbolic way of a Byzantine mosaic, or as the Face on the Shroud of Turin, which seems timeless and not done by any human artist.

• • •**Q** *As a philosopher, what aspect of Christ's personality appeals to you the most?*

• • •**A** The mystery of it. The fact that there's always something more there than you can lay your hands on and classify; the fact that he's different than any other human being that you ever met. And, at the same time, the total universality and humanness and identifiability of Christ. It's like the human face—it's endlessly interesting, you never get bored with it—and yet it's right there on the surface for a child to see. An absolutely unique blend of intricate profundity and simplicity.

• • •**Q** *In your own reading of Scripture and praying with Scripture, which texts do you like best, which verses do you keep going back to?*

• • •**A** I think the most profound section in all of Scripture is John 17, that intimate prayer between Jesus and his Father. We're allowed there to eavesdrop on the very conversation of the Trinity. One of my favorite parts of Scripture is Psalm 51, the "Sinner's Psalm."

And the most fascinating part of Scripture for me is the book of Revelation—precisely because I don't understand it. Of all the scenes in the Gospel, though, I guess the most moving has to be the crucifixion, because that shows how much God loves me.

• • •**Q**   *When did you feel that the crucifixion became a sense of focus for you?*

• • •**A**   No one big dramatic moment, but I do remember that when I was very young (maybe twelve years old), I saw a religious picture of Christ on the cross. It was the traditional crucifix with the inscription underneath, "I did this for you, what have you done for me?" That was challenging for me—who loved the New York Giants more than God—who, until then, had never been moved by a religious image.

• • •**Q**   *Can you describe your relationship with Jesus today?*

• • •**A**   I would say "incredibly inadequate." It's like the relationship between a flea and an elephant. A very strange love affair, indeed—that an elephant would condescend to love the flea!

• • •**Q**   *Do any titles of Jesus—friend, teacher, master— have a particular appeal to you?*

• • •**A**   That's like asking, "What's your favorite Psalm?" It depends on where I am and what my need is. If I'm going through hard times, the friend who's got his hand out for my hand is crucial. If I'm reading Scripture then the teacher is crucial. One of the things we have to learn, and it's hard to learn, is the art of focusing on the appropriate aspect of the truth that we need at the time. For instance, when we're tempted to sin, we usually think of God as very forgiving. And when we sin, we usually see God in terms of justice. But we need to do exactly the opposite. We need to remember the iron law of justice *before* we sin, and we have to realize the infinite mercy *afterwards*. So the art consists in finding the right aspect of God, and the right relationship with God, through Christ. That's an ongoing and difficult process.

• • •**Q** *Was there ever a moment in your life when your awareness of Christ's presence hit you more strongly, the awareness that he'd been there the whole time and it just became more intense?*

• • •**A** At a number of critical points in my life (for instance, when I thought my daughter was going to die and I was, in a human way, totally out of control) I got an assurance that didn't come from my own weak nature and a strange calm that I didn't expect—I knew that came from Christ. When I became a Catholic I experienced the feeling, as well as the conviction, that this Church was home, that Christ lived here. In my experiences with the Charismatic Renewal the pale light became a fire—which needs a fireplace. But the fireplace needs a fire, too—that's another aspect of the truth.

• • •**Q** *How do you express your relationship with Christ? Do you have any particular method of prayer?*

• • •**A** Well, reading Scripture, certainly, and spontaneous prayer. I find that I'm so lazy that I usually need to verbalize—I'm a real scatterbrain. I think I'm also congenitally Catholic in that I love liturgy and ceremony and ritual and repetition. I love the Rosary and the Psalms.

• • •**Q** *What do you like about the Rosary?*

• • •**A** It's like a magic spell that unwinds. We're conditioned not only by conscious thought but also by repetition. Advertising knows that; the more you can drill a message in, the more conditioned we are to it. The Rosary is a good repetition. To hear those words, those holy words, over and over again is like music. It puts a kind of harmony in the soil so that the plants can grow better. I think one reason I like the Rosary is that it's one thing I can do. If I were capable of great mystical prayer I might not need it. But it's a crutch and I'm a cripple; I need it.

• • •Q   *There's the Catholic maxim "to Jesus through Mary." Have you found that to be true in your devotion to Mary and the Rosary.*

• • •A   Yes, to have help from friends in high places is good both on earth and in heaven!

• • •Q   *If Jesus were to come back to earth today, what question would you like to ask him? What conversation would you like to have with Jesus?*

• • •A   I guess I would just be dumb and silent like Job. Job had a thousand questions to ask God...and when God finally showed up he didn't ask a one of them.

• • •Q   *Peter, what would say have been the most grace-filled moments of your life?*

• • •A   Somebody once asked me which of my books (I've written about twenty-four of them) did I think was the best one in God's eyes? And I said it was the one I never wrote because I was staying home to help my wife take care of the kids when they were little. The same holds true here. Which was my most grace-filled moment? It was the moment that I wasn't striving for grace, feeling grace, or reaching after it. It was when I was just humbly doing God's will. In the New Testament there are a lot of verses that say: hold fast, keep the faith. I think that ordinary daily fidelity is grace-filled, even if great moments don't shine out. The same holds true in marriage: the most important things are not the spectacular things, not the great moments, not the honeymoon, but fidelity. None of this seems very dramatic, but it is the greatest drama of all.

Archbishop James Lyke, OFM,
Ph.D., has served as a high school
teacher, pastor, Newman chaplain,
and as auxiliary bishop of Cleveland,
Ohio. In June of 1991, he was
installed as Archbishop of the diocese
of Atlanta, Georgia.

JAMES LYKE, OFM

● ● ●**Q** *Bishop Lyke, how do you picture Jesus, his looks,
the expression on his face? When you pray and call to mind
the image of Jesus, who do you see?*

● ● ●**A** I don't consciously choose nor spontaneously
have an image of Jesus when I pray. I simply try to
place myself in God's presence.

● ● ●**Q** *How do you experience the presence of Christ?*

● ● ●**A** A pre-eminent way in which I experience the
presence of Christ is in the context of the Eucharist,
where we recall the great acts of God and the principal
act of Christ, his Son, in the passion, death and resurrection. It is difficult for me to say much beyond that. I can
say, however, that in my own life and growth it has
been very important for me to understand that Jesus is
both the cosmic, universal Christ, as well as the Christ
of my heritage.

● ● ●**Q** *Can you explain that a bit?*

● ● ●**A** Well, we know that art typically depicts Jesus
in patterns that are appropriate to the ethnic and racial
background of the artist. And while that has been a very
natural process for the broader European community, it

has not been the case within the African-American community. We were reared in a society that is fundamentally racist, and as a result, even to this day, many of our people do not understand the sense of a Black Christ. Yet, Pope John Paul II once said to the people of Africa, "In Africa, Christ is African." In other words, the human person on the one hand feels the reality of the cosmic and universal Christ, but knows also that this Christ lifts one in one's human concreteness and in the day to day reality of one's life. In that sense, Christ is African, African-American, Irish, Italian and so on, because Christ always addresses people in their concrete reality. Christ blesses the dignity of the person in that person's concrete reality—which for me is African-American.

• • •**Q**   *In St. Paul we read that Christ made himself all things to all people, is that something of the same concept?*

• • •**A**   Well, it's certainly a good portion of the concept—it's a good statement to use if it's properly understood. You see, when Paul says, "Christ has become all things to all people," it's a Pauline way of saying that Christ is available to everyone. When Paul made that statement I don't think he was thinking of ethnicity as such. He was thinking of how Christ could be appropriated in all human concreteness. So Christ on the one hand transcends all human circumstances, and on the other hand is accessible to every human being—no matter what the circumstances of their life.

• • •**Q**   *How do you understand Christ's personality, his character? And from all that the Gospel gives us, which aspects of his person most appeal to you?*

• • •**A**   I really don't allow any one aspect to appeal to me more than another. When Christ reveals himself in

Sacred Scripture, particularly in the Gospels, he gives as much of the totality of himself as is divinely possible and humanly understandable. Since everything is divinely possible but not everything is humanly understandable, the human mind can only grow point by point, and day by day, until life is over and one's appropriation of Christ is complete. In a sense, it's a mistake to try to lean on one image, because if I do that then I block out other possibilities, the richness and depth of other images. However, at different points in my life a particular application may be helpful and timely. For example, because of my particular vocation in life, the image of the Good Shepherd is appealing. But, although I'm a priest (and the priesthood is a very essential part of my life), I am first of all a Christian. So, the Christ who drives the money changers out of the temple is also important to me, because as a member of the Christian community I must stand over and against all the evil that's in the temple, so to speak, of society.

• • •**Q** *In Scripture, is there any one passage that you would consider to be the most challenging or relevant for today's society?*

• • •**A** I would say again that one must be careful in focusing in on a particular passage to the detriment of others. Having said that, however, I would choose "Christ is our peace," from Ephesians. All my life, as a result of being a Black person here in the United States, and seeing the terrible need for unity and harmony within the human family, I have read that text as a particular and challenging call from Christ: "But now in Christ Jesus, you that used to be so far off have been brought close, by the blood of Christ. For he is the peace between us and he has made the two into one entity and broken down the barrier which used to keep them apart.... He came to bring the good news of peace to you who were far off and peace to those who were near. Through him, then, we both in the one Spirit have free access to the Father" (cf Eph 2:13-15; 17-18).

• • •**Q** *Are there any texts that you feel are just for you?*

• • •**A** I honestly don't have that experience. I think that the text, "I am the way, the truth and the life" (cf Jn 14:6) summarizes it. And I can cite that text as an all-encompassing statement of Christ. Every other Scripture quote, every other image of Christ, can in a sense be related to those words of Jesus, "I am the way, the truth and the life."

• • •**Q** *And of all the different titles of Jesus, is there one that appeals to you more than the others? One that speaks to you about your personal relationship with Jesus?*

• • •**A** No. I prefer to approach my prayer life and my active life on the basis of the Word of God and the Sacred Liturgy. I believe that's how we need to train ourselves as Christian people. God has given us his Word and, let me put it another way, God has given us Christ Jesus as the very embodiment of the Divine. And what God has given us in Christ Jesus through Scripture and through the Sacraments (particularly the Eucharist) and through the Church, is over-arching for me. To me that's fundamental and primary. And however I construct my life of prayer and action, everything has to be grounded in those realities.

• • •**Q** *How, then, would you describe your own personal prayer?*

• • •**A** I believe strongly that prayer is primarily listening, and I believe we best converse with Christ when we read Scripture. Still, when I pray I often use something that was taught me by the Benedictine sisters in our grade school, and the words aren't from Scripture. It's, "Sacred Heart of Jesus, I implore the grace to love Thee ever more and more." That's my prayer.

• • •Q   *When did you first have an awareness of a relationship with Jesus?*

• • •A   For me, as for African-American families in general, relationship with Jesus began very early. My mother brought me up that way; she often sang spirituals and religious songs. I was brought up with a sense that God was in the home. God was everywhere and God called us to follow Jesus. God calls us to a life of compassion and understanding. All those things began early, in the home, and I simply grew into a better understanding of them and learned more and more how Jesus could become a part of my life. It's something not mapped out. It's something that, in some ways, happens as you move from childhood and your mother's apron strings into young adulthood and maturity.

• • •Q   *And was the call to the priesthood something that you struggled with, or was it a natural outgrowth of the environment that you grew up in?*

• • •A   For me, it was a natural outgrowth of my environment. The call to priesthood happened as a result of the example of the associate pastor of my home parish, St. George's, in Chicago. I simply saw how good, kind and dedicated he was. I experienced all of that in his relationship with my family, and I thought that I'd like to be like him. I think God used him, a diocesan priest, in a very key way to lead me into my vocation.

• • •Q   *And why did you become a friar-priest?*

• • •**A**   I became a friar-priest because the Franciscans used to hear confessions at my parish. Their ministry led me to do some reading about St. Francis, whom I began to see as a unique saint in the Christian family—one who's ideals resonated well within my own heart. St. Francis was a really perfect image of Christ for me. And yet, in some ways he was very much like me. I mean, he faced the ups and downs of life. He was very human, passionate, a sinner even—certainly he wasn't born a saint. And I can relate to that. But he also had a particular vision as to how everything is part of the family of God: the unity of creation, the dignity of the human person, the urgency for peace and justice, the sense of the poor and our responsibility to humankind. That's why many movements, so many varied movements, see St. Francis as their patron. With almost any social concern or worry, you can look at Francis and say, "He's the one who can show us the way." Similarly, with a contemplative nature or vocation you can look at Francis, see the profound sense of contemplation in his life, and find in him a role model and a patron.

• • •**Q**   *Could you share with us some personal experience when Jesus touched your life in a special and certain way?*

• • •**A**   I can give you three experiences! The first was in the summer of 1968 while I was making a Better World Retreat. I met a priest from a diocese in Chile who was obviously a mystic. His bishop had only two priests in the entire diocese, but had said, "I'll keep one of my priests for myself and I'll give the other to the world"—allowing this saintly priest to be involved in the Better World Movement. I was concelebrating Mass with him when a terrible sense of awe came over me. I was so aware of the deep experience that was his as he offered Mass that a real sense of Christ's presence came over me. In the chapel there was an awareness of Christ. And on his face I could see a real glow.

The second experience was also in 1968, when I met Dorothy Day. To see the power of this woman, her utter fidelity, deep sense of prayer and commitment to people—just to be around her was a powerful experience.

• • •Q *And the third experience?*

• • •A The third time was when I had the opportunity to be with Dr. Martin Luther King privately, for just about fifteen minutes. It was in Cleveland, I think in the fall of 1967. At the close of a meeting we ended up in the same room together—alone—and I just had a sense of the greatness of the man and how God was using him as a prophet for our times.

• • •Q *The last question is about you. How does Jim Lyke personally keep alive and nurture his relationship with Jesus?*

• • •A I'm not sure that I have a favorite prayer or specific methods....

• • •Q *What is it that helps you to foster and nurture your relationship with Christ?*

• • •A Well, I think Christ addresses us in every circumstance of our lives. He speaks to us even in our sinful inclinations and sins because they help us see the utter awesomeness of who God is, who Christ is, who the Spirit is. And every day is a new opportunity because Christ is so embedded in the realities and circumstances of our lives. I've gained a sense of the presence of God, and when I recall the imminence of the transcendent God in my life, it becomes obvious how God is such a part of everything. For example, I once had a deep conversation with a person who had to reveal certain things to me. And during our conversation I discovered so much of the presence of God, and I was aware that God was saying a lot more to me about myself than about the person who was speaking with me.

• • •**Q** *Do you always have a sense of peace?*

• • •**A** I have, and I'm saying this honestly, peace even in the midst of my own limitations, faults, failures and sins. Why? How? Because I'm firmly convinced that God accepts me as I am and that God will help me grow. And that God does not discriminate against me because of my weakness. Of all that, I'm firmly convinced.

*A former high school religion teacher and
campus minister, writer and international leader
in the Catholic Charismatic Renewal, and
mother of four, Patti Mansfield presently works
with the Catholic Charismatic Renewal of New
Orleans and its annual Southern Regional
Conference. She has authored several books,
including* As By a New Pentecost: the Dramatic Beginning of the Catholic Charismatic
Renewal *(Franciscan University Press), which
is currently being translated into French,
Spanish, Italian and Portuguese.*

PATTI MANSFIELD

• • •**Q**   *Patti, when would you say that your personal relationship with Jesus really began? Was it at the famous "Duquesne Weekend"?*

• • •**A**   As a Catholic, I believe that my personal relationship with Jesus began at Baptism, and has been nourished through the Eucharist, Confirmation, Reconciliation, Marriage, family life and catechetical training. However, I'm convinced that you can have a personal relationship with Jesus without allowing him to be the Lord of your life! The challenge I faced on the "Duquesne Weekend" was to surrender my whole life—every relationship, every concern, every aspect of it—to the Lordship of Jesus Christ. To place everything in my life—my thoughts, desires, vocation, every-thing—under his rule. So often we tend to pray only when in trouble, or we thank God when there's a special favor granted. It's so easy to confine Jesus to a place somewhere off to the side and pull him in when needed, or convenient, and on our own terms.

• • •**Q**   *What exactly was the "Duquesne Weekend" all about?*

• • •**A**   It was a weekend retreat of students from

Duquesne University in February of 1967 when the gifts of the Holy Spirit were poured out "as by a new Pentecost." It has come to mark the beginning of the Charismatic Renewal in the Roman Catholic Church. For me, it was a moment of deeper conversion, of an adult commitment to Christ and a release of the power and gifts of the Holy Spirit. The fundamental change that took place during that retreat was a realization that I had never really made an unconditional surrender to Jesus as the Lord of my life. I believed that he was the Son of God, but in terms of my personal relationship with him, I was still asking him to do my will, bless my plans, and to do things according to my time table. At the "Duquesne Weekend" I was confronted for the first time in my life by what it means to follow Jesus unconditionally...to be a disciple...to be a witness.

• • •Q   *And now, many years later, you're an author, lecturer, leader in the Catholic Charismatic Renewal—how do you see the person of Christ? How do you envision him?*

• • •A   I find the image of the Sacred Heart of Jesus very compelling because it is such a clear depiction of his love for us. But I don't usually have any visual image of him in mind when I pray. I hear him speak through Scripture in prayer, but it's not in an audible voice. Instead, there is an interior sense of his word coming to me, person to person. I also find myself drawn more and more to the image of Jesus on the cross, the crucifix. So much so that when I go into a church that doesn't have a crucifix in it I feel an emptiness.... I find it helpful in prayer to have a crucifix that I can hold in my hand and look at, especially in times of suffering. I unite my small sacrifices to the supreme sacrifice of Jesus Christ. Looking at the cross helps me believe in God's love.

• • •Q *And what about his personality? Each of us has a different understanding of it, from the Good Shepherd to Jesus turning over the money changers' tables. How do you understand Jesus' personality?*

• • •A We need to know the person of Christ as he really is. As I went through college I found that, although I was growing in an intellectual understanding of the Lord, what I was really hungering for was a greater knowledge of him—an experience of his presence. I didn't want to *know about him*, I wanted *to know him*. The image of Jesus the Good Shepherd brings out so beautifully the possibility of an intimate knowledge of Jesus Christ for every believer. Jesus says, "I know my own sheep. They follow me and hear my voice." That text from John 10, the image of Jesus as the Good Shepherd, reveals so much of his personal love for each of us. To me he is love incarnate...merciful love.

• • •Q *Patti, are there other images of Jesus from the Scriptures that you relate to?*

• • •A Yes, another Scriptural image that I love is that of the Bridegroom. The Song of Songs speaks eloquently of the love relationship of every soul with Jesus. He is Lord and Master of everything, the great God of the whole universe, yet he draws me to experience his tender, personal love, just as a bride knows the love of her bridegroom.

• • •Q *You are obviously very familiar with the Bible, which texts are the most challenging and comforting for you?*

• • •A Right now I find the most challenging is, "If anyone loves me he must take up his cross daily and follow me. He who loves his life will lose it" (cf Lk 9:23-24). Learning to forget myself, to daily take up my cross and follow Jesus is a constant challenge. In terms of comforting, I think of Jesus' words, "Come to me, all you who labor and are heavily laden and I will refresh you. Take my yoke upon you and learn from me, for I am gentle and humble of heart. My yolk is easy, my burden light" (cf Mt 11:28-30). He really does refresh us by his presence.

• • •**Q**   *Are there times when you've experienced more strongly that sense of the Lord's presence?*

• • •**A**   Yes, of course. The Duquesne Weekend was one such experience, when I was baptized in the Holy Spirit. But there is also the wonderful reality that Jesus is with me no matter what the circumstances, whether I'm on a mountain top or in a valley, when things are going my way and when they're not. The experience of having Jesus with me—the companionship of Jesus—is what makes life all worthwhile. If I'm suffering, then it's in union with him. If I'm rejoicing, then I acknowledge that he's the giver of gifts and has been good to me. For the past few years I've experienced a very special season of grace—a time of renewed intimacy with God. He's been showing me again in prayer, and in providing for certain needs in my family, how much he wants to be involved in my life, how much he loves me, how beautifully he cares for me. And this he desires to do for *all* his people.

• • •**Q**   *How do you nurture your relationship with the Lord? Is there any particular form of prayer that you find helpful?*

• • •**A**   Quiet, contemplative prayer is a gift...to "be still and know that he is God" (cf Ps 46). And the Eucharist is also very important in my life. Prayer before the Blessed Sacrament has always been a source of grace. With a family of four children and a busy life, I no longer have the luxury of uninterrupted hours of prayer before the Blessed Sacrament. Still, attendance at Mass and adoration of the Blessed Sacrament are like an oasis for me. I pray the Divine Office every day—it's something I've been doing for quite a few years now and I find it a tremendous help. I also try to visit my spiritual director monthly so that I'm able to make my confession and receive the guidance and discernment of a wise and holy priest.

• • •**Q** *And what about the forms of prayer usually associated with the Charismatic Renewal?*

• • •**A** The Charismatic Renewal has had a tremendous impact on my spiritual formation, and the prayer of praise and worship characterizes the Charismatic Renewal. In my own personal prayer I try to spend some time just praising and worshiping God, using the gift of tongues. I find the gift of tongues a tremendous aid in helping me to come into the presence of God. It is a gift for praising God when, as St. Paul says, "We know not how to pray" (cf Rom 8:26), and it also is a powerful means of offering intercession.

• • •**Q** *What about Mary and the saints?*

• • •**A** Mary is our Mother and the saints are our friends! I experience their help all the time. St. Therese of Lisieux has been like a sister to me since childhood and I've been influenced by her "little way." I also love St. Teresa of Avila, St. Joseph, St. Catherine, and Padre Pio. Spiritual reading, knowing the saints and experiencing their intercession, is an invaluable assistance for growing in holiness. I have consecrated my life to the Immaculate Heart of Mary, using the consecration composed by St. Louis de Montfort. Echoing the motto of Pope John Paul II, each day I say to Mary, "Totus

Tuus—I am all yours, Mary." Entrustment to Mary is a
tremendous means of spiritual growth and I would
recommend it to anyone seeking to deepen their union
with God. My own spiritual life can be summed up by
saying it is by the Holy Spirit and Mary that Jesus is
being formed in me. My desire is to bring him forth in
word and deed to those around me.

• • •**Q**   *Patti, if Jesus were to come back to earth today,
what would you like him to say?*

• • •**A**   I find it hard to think about what he might say,
as though he were not already speaking today. For me,
Jesus is not simply an historical figure, someone from
long ago, uninvolved or unattached to our everyday
life. He is alive and present in his body, the Church. As
Catholics, we believe that Jesus speaks to us through
the Holy Father and the teaching of the Church. Having
made that point, I might add that what I think we need
to hear in the Church today is a call to repentance and
holiness. Modern men and women need to live repentant lives, to turn from selfishness and sin, to turn to
God. By this I don't mean a repentance that is gloomy,
but a repentance that leads to new life and joy. I believe
that this is what the world, and the Church, needs
desperately to hear. We need to stop compromising, to
acknowledge that we're sinners, that only God is God.
Whatever good we have, whatever accomplishments
we've achieved, is all God's gift to us. Apart from him
we can do nothing. Individually and as a people we
need to turn our hearts back to God in repentance, in
prayer, in humility, and in serving the needs of others
in love.

photo by Jonas

An expert in the area of lay forma-
tion and a professor of literature
and spirituality at Duquesne
University's Institute of Formative
Spirituality, Dr. Susan Muto
currently serves as the executive
director of the Epiphany Associa-
tion. Author and lecturer, she is
also a principal writer for the
United States Bishops' pastoral on
women's concerns.

SUSAN MUTO

• • •**Q** *Would you describe, in a nutshell, your ministry: who you are and what you do?*

• • •**A** For twenty-one years I worked at Duquesne University in Pittsburgh, helping to establish the graduate program in spiritual formation. At first I was a lecturer in literature and spirituality. Later, I concentrated on teaching the literature of spirituality. In 1980, I was named director of the Institute of Formative Spirituality, succeeding Fr. Adrian Van Kaam. In 1988, I was invited to be executive director of the Epiphany Association, an ecumenical non-profit organization specializing in publication, consultation and research development fostering Christian formation. As a single lay woman, I felt strongly that I was called to the area of lay ministry. Now, my full time position in the Association enables me to live out that call.

• • •**Q** *With all of your educational and experiential background, who is Jesus now for you? When you pray, what image do you have of him?*

• • •**A** Interestingly enough, Van Dyke's image of Jesus, "In the Garden of Gethsemane," is much like my own. Because of my Italian roots—and also having been in the Holy Land—I picture Jesus as a person with a certain Mediterranean look. That is how Van Dyke pictured him. Christ's face is elegant and calming: his eyes are dark and inner-directed. One is drawn into the consciousness of Jesus' own maturing process. I think that my imaging of Jesus is that of a mature, Mediterranean man who has a warmth about him that simply draws one in and toward him.

• • •**Q**   *How would you then describe Jesus' personality, the kind of person he was?*

• • •**A**   I think I would use words that signify a certain rhythm of living words like gentle and firm, forthright and modest. I picture him in essence as a full personality, whole, strong and assertive, fully masculine yet perceptive and sensitive and, therefore, fully feminine. I really see him as *the* perfectly whole human being, psychologically and spiritually speaking. Also I'd mention the blending in Jesus of the man who was obedient to his mother's wishes at Cana, and yet who challenged the pharisees in a sharp and clever way, and who dealt angrily with the money changers in the temple. So I'm drawn to Jesus' personality as one that is totally balanced—not extreme in any direction, neither overly introverted nor overly extroverted.

• • •**Q**   *So, your Jesus is a versatile person?*

• • •**A**   Yes. I see Jesus as a person who could converse with the learned and the poor and be comfortable in both situations. I see him as one who knew when it was time to leave the crowds and go away to seek silence. In that sense, Jesus is someone I turn to when I find my own personality getting out of balance, when I become too involved with my ministry and I tend to neglect the call to go quietly apart.

• • •**Q**   *When you read through the New Testament, which of his words do you find most comforting and challenging?*

• • •**A**   I would begin with the words I use most frequently as a text for my own meditation and prayer: "Come to me, all you who labor and are heavy burdened and I will give you rest" (cf Mt 11:28-29). Those three words, "Come to me," are so important. The same with the words addressed to the apostles, "Follow me." Jesus' imperatives are, in general, intriguing to me. "Come to me" and "Follow me" are direct addresses. They are words that pierce through all of the layers of things that are not important. They really touch the heart.

• • •**Q**   *And the most challenging words...?*

• • •**A**   The most challenging words of Jesus are for me those associated with parables and stories. For example, the parable of the bridesmaids, with its "be on the alert." Again, that's another challenging imperative. There are many times when I'm asleep and I'm not on the alert, times when I live too much in forgetfulness of God's call and invitation. In the parable about the sower and seed, I'm reminded that the seed doesn't always fall on good ground. I think the story of Jesus and the young man offers an enormous challenge: do we understand it literally to mean that we must sell what we have and give it to the poor? What does that mean? Are we to take it at face value? Or are we to understand it as detaching ourselves from all that represents riches (our idols) to us?

• • •**Q**   *Is there any particular Gospel quote which you feel is speaking directly to you, to Susan?*

• • •**A**   I would have to go back to Jesus' farewell discourse in St. John's Gospel. That holds really an endless treasure. And, for me, there's no doubt that it always comes back to the point of "love one another as I have loved you" (cf Jn 13:34). I think there's nothing as important in the whole world, and John of the Cross echoes this revelation with his wonderful saying, "In the evening of life you will be judged on love."

• • •**Q** *Susan, how would you describe your own personal relationship with Jesus? Do you think of him as teacher, healer, rescuer, friend, Lord, God...?*

• • •**A** Of all the possible titles that appeal to me, the one I treasure most is Jesus as friend. My sense is that we have lost in our world an understanding of the art and discipline of spiritual friendship. Men and women don't know how to relate on the spiritual level all that well. Sometimes we get so caught up in our sensuality that we forget our spirituality and our need for spiritual friendship. I think that Jesus as friend is also important to me, as a woman. He had friends. He was loving to Mary and Martha. He said, "I call you friend; you are no longer slaves or servants, you are friends" (cf Jn 15:15). So I would say that Jesus as friend is central to me.

• • •**Q** *Is there a particular time in your life when you became aware of that friendship with Jesus?*

• • •**A** It goes back to my first grade teacher, Sr. Gemma, a Sister of St. Joseph and truly a gem. She was one of those delightful, simple souls who radiated love and radiated Christ. Over and over again she told us that, no matter what happened, "We could go on and talk to Jesus!" That was her whole philosophy. No matter what happened, we could talk to Jesus as we would to our best friend. So, Jesus is my friend, the one with whom I can really talk over anything and everything that happens and that is going on in my life. He is someone who will stand by me through thick and thin.

He will always be there to console, to forgive, and to encourage me to start over again.

• • •**Q**   *When did that relationship start to take on a special and significant meaning in your life?*

• • •**A**   I think it began to really click in when I was an undergraduate at Duquesne University. During those years I would often drop into the chapel and just sit there and know that Jesus was there for me—that he was a friend to whom I could turn. I became the editor of our student newspaper—I think I was the first female editor in years—and found that, because I had to remain above it all in order to be objective in my assessment of student issues, there was a lot of loneliness in that job. I think that it was out of the experience of loneliness that I began to understand that I would be less lonely if I had a relationship with Jesus. I would say that my relationship with Jesus began with that intuition. And over the years it has been confirmed....

• • •**Q**   *Could you share any of those moments when Jesus touched your life in a special way?*

• • •**A**   It's hard to verbalize religious experiences... and because I'm cursed, or blessed, with years of study of John of the Cross, I really want to say, "Nada, Nada, Nada." I don't want to spoil anything by putting it into human words, or making it more important or more dramatic than it really was. I believe we have to be discrete about these things. But, at the times when I have suffered loneliness, misunderstanding, or physical suffering, when I have felt betrayed by my human circle of co-workers or colleagues, at those times it has seemed to me that Jesus has come into my heart with great love and tenderness, assuring me of his friendship, assuring me that there was some meaning to this suffering, that I would grow through it and that by passing beyond it I would come to know him better.

• • •Q   *If Jesus were to come back to earth today and appear on prime time television, what topic would you like him to speak about?*

• • •A   I think I would want Jesus to address the question of spiritual hunger, particularly how lay people can satisfy their need for in-depth, ongoing formation. I would want him to help us to understand that without a personal relationship with God we will be continually caught up in, what I might call, a substitute for the transcendent. To understand that without him we will be lost in our addictions and abusive behaviors and not be able to find our way through them to freedom. I guess I would want him to give us guidance, a sense of how we are to be in the world but not of it, and how we are to act when surrounded by temptations like hedonism, consumerism and narcissism....

• • •Q   *How do you nurture and express your relationship with Jesus Christ?*

• • •A   The nurturing comes to me through the common ways of Catholic spirituality: liturgy, sacraments, and especially the Eucharist. I think my relationship with Jesus is nurtured, in a privileged way, by the fact that I am a teacher in the field of spirituality. My work obliges me to read the literature of spirituality, to study the writings of great masters—Augustine, Benedict, Teresa of Avila, John of the Cross, Therese of Lisieux, and many contemporaries. I also think that we are becoming more and more a lay church, and so have to find ways of enhancing lay formation that will tie in with the lay person's life. The big mistake has been (and I say this with all due respect for the tradition which I certainly love and study), to impose a monastic, or a clerical, or a conventual model on lay people as their way to God. That imposition harbors built-in guilt because lay women are not mini-nuns, and laymen are not mini-clerics or mini-monks. Hence, we have to develop models of formation that will be appropriate for the vocations of parenting, marriage, single life, etc. That will require some new resources, but if we can find a way of communicating in-depth formation by means of TV, video, and audio, as well as books, so much the better. Maybe in due time we will find the secret of living in the world while not being entirely of the world!

A Trappist monk, Fr. Basil Pennington, OCSO, is a well-known and popular author and lecturer, often credited with helping the Catholic Church in America take a new look at centering prayer and redefine its contemplative dimension.

BASIL
PENNINGTON, OCSO

• • •**Q** *Father, when you close your eyes in prayer, can you describe the image you get of Jesus?*

• • •**A** I would say that at this point in my life I don't get an image. I think of Jesus and me being one; there's no separation—I have no image.

• • •**Q** *So you have an awareness of the presence of Jesus rather than a mental image of him?*

• • •**A** Yes. When I let things go and am simply present to what is, then I know that Jesus and I are one.

• • •**Q** *If I asked you to think of Jesus in his humanity, and to consider his personality, how would you describe it? What kind of man was he?*

• • •**A** Extremely attractive, compassionate, the kind of person you like to be with. He gives you the space to be—without judgment or expectations, without putting you into a category. He accepts you as you are and loves you totally. In his presence you can rejoice in who you are and feel the power of his healing and of his love—and know that everything's taken care of.

• • •**Q** *When you read through Scripture, which passage* *do you feel very comfortable with and enjoy hearing over and over again?*

•••A   Well, my favorite section is in John, at the Last Supper, when Jesus speaks about his infinite oneness with us and his love for us, and of how much his Father loves us. He's pouring out his heart in that text, and trying to say what, for any lover, is really inexpressible. I listen to that again and again, and it forms my mind and body and spirit.

•••Q   *How would you describe your own personal relationship with Jesus? Would you consider him more as a teacher, healer, friend, brother, Lord, God?*

•••A   Friend! but in it's fullest sense—lover! By that, I understand oneness; he is the image of true love between husband and wife. But that image itself doesn't even express it fully. What I'm trying to express is that we're one. Everything that concerns me concerns him, and everything that concerns him concerns me. We feel and think and love alike.

•••Q   *You were nineteen when you joined the Trappists. Can you tell us about your spiritual journey? When did you come to an awareness of Jesus' presence in your life?*

•••A   Well, Jesus was present in our home through family prayer—we said the Rosary daily—but it wasn't just at prayer time. Jesus was really present as part of the family, and we wanted to please him and be with him and do what he wanted. We went to Mass every day; we would serve Mass and celebrate the Church feasts and so on....

•••Q   *So, you were kind of surrounded by the Faith?*

•••A   Yes. Jesus was present in our home as some-one who loved and cared for us. He was there as part of the family, someone to whom we could turn to and count on—he and his mother. As a young person I became an altar boy, then sacristan and master of ceremonies. I lived the liturgical life intensely. On holy days, and especially each Holy Thursday, Good Friday and Holy Saturday, all day was spent in church—the whole week was totally taken up with Jesus, living this mystery of the Passover. Then through the years, of course, it's been very important to sit with the Gospels... that's where Jesus talks to us. He always says the same thing, but he says it more deeply and it makes more of an impact on your life. And sometimes, even though you've read the Gospel many times, he says things that you just never heard before—and it's a new experience.

• • •**Q**   *Did that home atmosphere influence your choosing a religious vocation? Can you tell us something of your vocation story?*

• • •**A**   Well, just as with every kid who was brought up as I was, I felt drawn to the priesthood. But I decided that the diocesan priesthood wasn't enough; I wanted something more. I began looking at missionary orders...I wanted to feed the whole world.

• • •**Q**   *Obviously you didn't make it into a missionary community! What happened?*

• • •**A**   Somehow the Lord told me to wait. But I still had that desire to feed the whole world, and I also had a very personal desire for a deep and close union with him. There was also a certain amount of what one would call "spiritual ambition." In those days we thought of one religious order as "better" than another, and the Trappists were supposed to be the very best. But the great desire was to be one with Christ and to save the whole world. And, you know, God always gives you what you want, but he doesn't always give it the way you expect it. He gives it to you in ways that are far more wonderful.

• • •**Q**   *Fr. Basil, you mentioned saying the Rosary as a child. How does Mary fit into your spiritual journey?*

• • •**A**   In the Holy Year of 1950 I gave myself to the Blessed Mother. I probably did it many times before that, but 1950 was the time when I *really* did it. And I know she has kept me close to her Son. St. Anne is important in my life, too. At the suggestion of my spiritual director, who opposed my Trappist vocation, I went to seek confirmation of my vocation at the Shrine of St. Anne de Beaupre in Canada. And when I got home my spiritual director had been transferred a hundred miles away!

• • •**Q**   *That's great! Father, have there been times over the years when your relationship with Jesus was a little rocky, when you had to recharge the battery of your desires, so to speak?*

• • •**A**   In my relationship with the Lord there's never been anything like that. It's just been a deepening, growing relationship. At times he's come to me in a very special way.... My first spiritual father was a Trappist—a great contemplative, a very holy man—and his spiritual father was Dom Marmion. He used to say to me, "Marmion, he was always in the light and I'm always in the dark." Of course, Marmion had his struggles, too. (Once he admitted that he was tired of Mass; he had to fight the temptation to lie down on the floor of his stall!) But he'd always been in the light. And I think I've always been in the light...it's never been dark.

• • •**Q**   *Can you share any of those times when Jesus has*

*made himself present to you in a special or extraordinary
way?*

● ● ●**A**   Yes, there was a time when I had taken a
sabbatical to stay six months at Mount Athos, and then
went on to France to spend two months with a great
spiritual father there. I spent almost the whole time in
one little room. One day, on the feast of St. Aelred, I
was reading Aelred's treatise on friendship and Jesus
came to me embraced me—and we became one.

● ● ●**Q**   *Can you explain that?*

● ● ●**A**   He was just there. Recently, the whole Trinity
just came. It's an experience. You let it be, let it do what
it wants and go on, you see.

● ● ●**Q**   *How do you live your spiritual life on an every day
level? When those special moments aren't present?*

● ● ●**A**   Well, the Mass is fantastic. Jesus gave us this
ritual within which we reach into the eternal now of
God and make Calvary—the greatest act of love—
present right here. In the Mass we can really be one
with Jesus, offer the Father praise, thanksgiving, adoration, reparation, everything that is due to him in a way
that's worthy. So the Mass is wonderful! Also, there are
times when I can't go apart and spend days in solitude
with Jesus, so I walk with him all the time. The first
time I was traveling by myself in Europe I met a couple
on the train in Italy, and they asked me, "Aren't you
lonely traveling by yourself?" And I stopped, and said,
"No, I have Jesus with me." It never dawned upon me
to be lonely.

● ● ●**Q**   *Father, can you say something about your experience of prayer? You're well known for your teaching of the
centering prayer method....*

● ● ●**A**   It's so important to teach people that they can pray always. That's one thing about the centering prayer, it's very simple. If someone's lying in bed sick and says, "I can't pray!" I tell them to just look at the crucifix and say, "Jesus!" Or I suggest that they hold the crucifix, a prayer stone, rosary...it's so simple. You don't have to do or say anything; just have the awareness that Jesus is there.

• • •**Q**   *There are so many techniques, but obviously the Holy Spirit is the best teacher of prayer....*

• • •**A**   I think the Holy Spirit is so mysterious, so very difficult for people to comprehend. I know I have a special relationship with the Holy Spirit, but it's so undefinable because it's totally spiritual. With Jesus I can speak about friend and lover and make some sense, and with the Father I can speak about God as Father. But all in all, the Holy Spirit is very difficult. That's why God became man, so man can become God. But I think often times when we talk about the Holy Spirit, and being open to the Holy Spirit or listening to the Spirit, it's incomprehensible for people. Instead, when you talk about Jesus it's easier. A person can open the Gospels, image Jesus being there, or image your most loving experiences...whether it's intimacy with a lover or something like that which a person can experience.

• • •**Q**   *What's the role of centering prayer in your relationship with Jesus? How did you start teaching it?*

• • •**A**   Well, our Lord himself taught me centering when I was very young. I would go to church, be with him, and use his Holy Name. When I entered the monastery we had a novice master who presumed we novices knew nothing about prayer. And he got out the old books and started with meditative prayer, reflective prayer...and it just didn't work for me. Later, I was asked to be the Vocation Father, and was sent to a vocation conference in Rome. During the conference someone asked, "How do you get across to a young person the idea of contemplative life?" A priest jumped up (he was a Salesian by the name of McCabe, from Brazil), and said the only way to get the idea of the contemplative life across to young people is to put them into it, lead them into the reality of it. So, I started the cottage program.

You see, it had become clear to me that in our guest house we were providing a place of silence and solitude, with good books and rest and food, but we weren't teaching people in any practical way how to enter into contemplative prayer. But contemplative prayer is our tradition from John Cassian on.... That's how it all started, with these young men who were coming to see what the contemplative life was about.

• • •**Q** *So, your teaching prayer really started with voca- tional direction?*

• • •**A** Yes. Then I was asked to do something for the superiors, and then for other religious, and so on. I was filling a practical need, and it was a great joy to help people open up to Jesus. I've always enjoyed teaching centering prayer. And it's funny, sometimes I'm teach- ing centering prayer and my own relationship with Jesus is just so-so while those I'm teaching are having these wonderful experiences. And I say, "Hey Lord, how about me?" But I see such transformations, and it's so powerful, especially in lay people—but also in priests and religious.

• • •**Q** *You must have had the opportunity to witness many special moments for people...?*

• • •**A** God does sometimes give us special experiences of himself. And they're wonderful things, and you live with them. Mary does the same. But special experiences are not the important thing. The important thing is just everyday living in intimate love of Jesus as friend, as lover. If people knew how much Jesus loved them, then the loneliness, the isolation and the walls, defensiveness, competition...all that would fade away. Someday we will know that the ones who were closest to Jesus, who were the greatest delights to his heart, and who did the greatest things in the world, were people nobody ever saw—like St. Joseph. That is why I have some hesitation in talking about my experiences. In a sense they're not very important, still I can never thank God enough for those experiences.... But Jesus wants to have a deep and intimate relationship with every person.

A professor of theology at Loyola University in Chicago, Fr. John Powell, SJ, is presently the second best-selling Christian author in the history of the United States, ranking just behind C.S. Lewis. From 1980 to 1985 his popular TV series, "American Catholic," reached an estimated nine million homes weekly and was the first national Catholic program since that of the late Archbishop Sheen.

JOHN POWELL, SJ

• • •**Q**   *Father, you have such an incredibly active life, during your moments alone with Christ, how do you see him? What type of person is Jesus for you?*

• • •**A**   I have on the wall of my room a picture of Jesus called the "Smiling Christ," and I always picture Jesus as someone who is happy and content. Most of the paintings and the portrayals I've seen have been of a very sad Jesus. But I imagine him as a smiling, happy, gentle person—someone who is firm and asks a lot of us, but who easily forgives our failings. I also think of Jesus as being very demanding. Jesus invites us into a relationship of love in which he demands a lot.

• • •**Q**   *Can you relate the love of Jesus and the demands of Jesus to particular passages of Scripture, perhaps favorite texts which comfort or challenge you?*

• • •**A**   The text that I find most comforting is the story of the prodigal son. That parable is the answer to the question of what God thinks of a sinner. And Jesus tells us in that wonderful story that God is always waiting for us with open arms. Jesus' command to be a loving person is the most challenging. I'm also challenged by St. Paul, who says to make love the rule of your life.

And I'm challenged by Jesus' words at the Last Supper about a life of service.

• • •**Q**   *What would you say is the essence of your personal relationship with Jesus? Is he teacher, healer, friend...?*

• • •**A**   I think he's more of a friend than a teacher. When I witness a marriage, as the bride and groom come down the aisle, I think to myself: how well do they know each other? My answer usually is: not very well. They're getting into a boat to take an uncharted journey—and I hope they're going to make it. It occurred to me that that's what the Lord is asking of us, that kind of commitment. We don't know what the future will hold; we don't know what we're going to be like in ten years.... But the Lord asks that we be committed to him, to sharing our lives with him.

• • •**Q**   *When would you say your own commitment and relationship with Jesus became a meaningful part of your life?*

• • •**A**   I think it started as I was growing up here in Chicago. At our Catholic High School we went to daily Mass, and I have always strongly believed in the Eucharistic Presence. Upon graduation from high school I prepared to enter a Jesuit seminary. Prior to leaving home I went across the street to say good-bye to a neighbor. When I told him I was going off to study for the priesthood, he became very serious and a stricken look crossed his face. Then he said, "But there is no God!" In no uncertain terms he told me that no God could preside over a world in which there was war. Later, I thought over our conversation and found it strange—until I entered the Jesuit novitiate. It was spartan, awful, and I thought, well, if there really is a God then this is God's boot-camp! But if there was no God, then, I couldn't think of a spookier way to spend my life. And this is exactly what my neighbor had said, "You're pouring your life down a drain; you've got so much talent, etc." So I went to the chapel and prayed... with no immediate results forthcoming. Then I went to the master of novices and told him that I thought I was an atheist. He said, "Um-hum." And I said, "Father, I don't think I believe in God." More um-hums, and a "be patient." So I thought, what am I suppose to be patient about? Four months later, just before going to bed, I felt God's presence deep inside me. I felt touched by God and I remember feeling like a balloon that was being blown up with ecstasy, pure joy. That feeling lasted for about three weeks, and it turned the novitiate into a heaven on earth. It was at that time, during my novitiate year, that God became real to me.

• • •**Q** *Father, having come through that very personal experience of doubts and questioning, if Jesus were to appear today on prime time television, what topic would you like him to address?*

• • •**A** I would ask him why only one quarter of the world is Christian. And then I'd ask about the other three quarters who have never heard of baptism, and don't know about him at all—what happens to them after death? Another question I'd like to ask him is about "faith." I know too many people who say, "Show me and then I'll believe." No! Jesus asks us to believe, and then he will show us. It's faith that releases the power of God. God is like an electrical outlet, you can heat a room, you can wash dishes, you can show movies, you can do almost anything...but you've got to get plugged in. And the plug in is faith. Or it's like this boy flying a kite: The kite was surrounded by low-flying clouds and a man passed by and said, "Hey, what's up there? How come you've got that string in your hand?"

The boy said, "I'm flying a kite." The man said, "I don't see a kite up there, how do you know there's a kite up there?" "Oh," the little boy said, "when I pull on the kite string I can feel it." I think, how do I know there's a God up there? I pull on the kite string. I've felt him; I know him.

• • •**Q**   *How do you nurture and express your relationship with Jesus?*

• • •**A**   I talk to him all day. I'm continually sharing my life with him. We laugh about some things, cry about some things, lament about persons and events. And I pray—before I write, go into a classroom, get up to give a speech—I always pray. And my prayer is: "Lord, don't let it be another performance, make it an act of love! I don't know who's out there. I don't know who will read this book. I don't know what I'm saying. But I ask you to guide me, to be my inspiration." So I nurture my own faith by sharing in dialogue directly with the Lord. I also receive a lot of affirmation from people who have heard some audio cassette or read one of my books and say, "You know, you've helped me a great deal, you've turned my life around." Isn't it marvelous that God would use me to help someone? I always pray, and somehow those prayers have paid off. Somehow God does choose to work through me.

• • •**Q**   *Do you have a particular method of formal prayer that you use?*

• • •**A**   Well, every day I start out by telling him who I am, what I've worried about most in the last twenty-four hours, what I've thought about...what is my biggest concern. I speak honestly to the Lord, because it's my belief that not even God can get through a mask, a barrier.

• • •**Q** *Father, are there any other moments when you felt that Jesus really touched your life in an extraordinary way?*

• • •**A** A real moment of grace came when I was scheduled to speak to the Loyola community of Jesuits. I wanted to impress them and I was very nervous—my mouth was dry, my hands were cold. I prayed for help, asking to be able to impress them, asking for poise, etc. But nothing happened. So I prayed, "Are you trying to tell me something?" And I swear that I heard these words in my imagination: "You are getting ready to give another performance." I know those words were from God because I would never embarrass myself like that. And the voice continued, "You're getting ready to give a performance. You're getting ready to perform for your brothers so they will know how good you are." And that was exactly what I had in mind. The voice continued, "I don't need any more performances from you—only acts of love! And your brothers need you to love them so they will know how good *they* are."

Well, I remember looking out at the Jesuit community (and I've always believed that empathy is the first step to loving), and I thought: Oh, God, I wonder what it's like to be old? I wonder what it's like to be retired? I wonder what it's like when you aren't pulling your weight or making a salary? I looked at the sick men and wondered what it feels like to have arthritis, or an ulcer, or headaches.... Then I looked out at the men in my community who were "failures," and I thought: I wonder what it's like to be a failure? I wonder what it's like when people laugh at you...when you never get invited out...I wonder what it's like? And then the men who were alcoholics—I wonder what it's like to be addicted? They go to AA meetings and they stand up and say, "My name is John and I'm an alcoholic." I wonder what that's like?

I looked out at the Jesuit community that night and said, "Brothers, have I ever loved you? I don't know, I really don't know. I'm nice to live with, I think, but I don't know if I have really loved you. For me, when you love another person you have to study that person. You have to ask, 'What do you need?' Have I loved you? God, I don't know!" That night I promised them that I would love them. At the end of my conference one Jesuit, who doesn't like lectures, said, "I was very impressed by what you had to say. I was moved by it." And that's when I discovered that when you are a loving person, God will act through you and touch others.

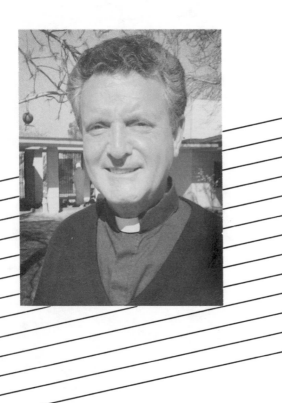

Originally from England, Fr. Kenneth Roberts, priest, evangelist, apostle of Mary, and author of his conversion story, Playboy to Priest, *continues to inspire thousands, especially the young, to commit themselves to Christ and the Church.*

KENNETH ROBERTS

• • •**Q** *Fr. Ken, you're well known as a man who was converted from the life of an international playboy to a fervent and dedicated priest, how have you come to image Jesus?*

• • •**A** At various times I see him differently, depending on my own mood. There are times when I see him as the Good Shepherd, especially when I'm looking for the lost sheep. There are times I see him as teacher, Lord, brother.... If I'm having a particularly bad day and everything's gone wrong, then I'm looking for Christ on the cross, or Christ in the garden. But on a good day, I see him having a good time, even partying. I see Christ laughing, taking time off with the apostles and saying, "Let's get away from it all." There are many facets to Jesus, and it depends on where I'm at. Mostly, perhaps, I see him as a brother.

• • •**Q** *And what about his personality?*

• • •**A** My favorite picture of Christ is Hook's "Jesus." And while I would say he has a strong personality, I think his character was soft and gentle. He could be forceful, especially as when he cleansed the temple, but most of the time I see him being gentle with the sinner and very firm and strong with the self-righteous.

• • •**Q**   *When you read Scripture, which passages do you read as most challenging?*

• • •**A**   The texts where Christ talks to the righteous. Especially to the people who were religious—to me, as a priest—as when Jesus said, "They loved the high places at table...they loved people to acknowledge them...to call them by titles..." (cf Mt 23:6). Sometimes I think, my God, that's me.

• • •**Q**   *And what passage do you find most comforting?*

• • •**A**   The one I find most comforting and preach most often is from St. Paul, when he says, "God made him who did not know sin to be sin, so that in him we might become the very holiness of God" (cf 2 Cor 5:21). I find that comforting for people like me who are great sinners, because we feel, "My God, I've been so sinful, I've been so wicked—how could God really forgive me?" And then we read that one line, "God took their sins and gave them his holiness, God made him who did not know sin to be sin, so that in him we might become the very holiness of God." It says everything; I've had people cry when telling them about it.

• • •**Q**   *Is there a passage in which you feel Jesus is speaking just for you?*

• • •**A**   "Come follow me. Leave everything, come follow me" (cf Mk 1:17).

• • •**Q**   *When did you realize that the Lord was speaking there to you?*

• • •**A**   It was something that haunted me for a long time. It's the story of my own conversion experience.... I was living the fast life, the rich life, traveling all over the world, when I met Mother Teresa's nuns in India. One of them was a young English girl who had given up everything to become a missionary. I asked her how she could be so happy living in all that filth. She looked me in the eye and asked how I could be happy living in *my* filth. And she told me that my life, in the eyes of God, was filthier than that city. That hurt, and I was very angry at her. But her words haunted me. I'd go to parties, and I kept hearing her voice and remembering what she'd said.

• • •**Q** *Was that the moment of your conversion?*

• • •**A** The final conversion came not long after that. I was in Beirut and had been invited to an all night party. I arrived rather late and everybody was drunk and an orgy (women and men, nakedness, people falling on the floor) was in full swing. I walked out—nauseous and disgusted with the human race. Later in the day I went for a walk and eventually into a Catholic Church where Benediction was being held—and that's where I experienced Christ. It was a born-again experience; a spirit-filled experience. And it was real, not just emotional. The priest told me to get out of that lifestyle or I'd be lost.

• • •**Q** *Is that when Christ became a meaningful part of your life?*

• • •**A** Yes, I guess it was at that time in Beirut during Benediction. I went into the Church and was struck—it was like a bible scene. All the men had long robes on, the women were dressed like the Virgin Mary. And as I looked around the church I understood how, although Arabic, it was Catholic. And I understood then what Catholic is—it's not English, or European—Catholic means all-embracing. These were my thoughts when suddenly I realized that the priest was holding up the Blessed Sacrament. The bell was ringing, and that's when I felt a tingling, a power, a shower of love. At that moment I felt like I'd been cleansed from the inside and was being filled with love and joy...and all the things that are great. I felt a great closeness to Christ at that moment.

• • •**Q**   *And from then on...?*

• • •**A**   From then on I started going to daily Mass and monthly confession; I made serious attempts at a prayer life. I still went to parties and led the rich life, but I didn't get drunk and I tried to avoid sin. I didn't always succeed, but I tried. And I continued doing that for a couple of years.

• • •**Q**   *When did you feel called to the priesthood?*

• • •**A**   It was while I was engaged and preparing for marriage. As the wedding date drew closer, I realized that I was, in fact, going to be a priest. It seemed ridiculous. So three weeks before the wedding I went to church, knelt before the Blessed Mother and prayed, "We're about to be married, so if you want me to be a priest you'd better intervene!" I went out for lunch with my fiancee, and during the meal she took off her engagement ring, put it on the plate and walked out. I was mad at God! I felt rejected. But I didn't enter the seminary, because I figured that if I entered right then people would say I was going in on the rebound. Then, I lost my job at British Airlines only to get a better job on the ocean-liner *Queen Elizabeth*. It seemed that whenever God was showing me one thing, there would always be an extra temptation added to keep me from going into the seminary.... And that's been the pattern of my life, really! It seems like it's a constant battle between good and evil. And all the while God is trying to teach me humility.

• • •**Q**   *How would you describe your relationship with Jesus?*

• • •**A**   My main relationship with Christ would be Eucharistic. I try to make a daily visit to the Blessed Sacrament, and not necessarily talk so much as be still. I just sit there, sometimes for twenty minutes, and do nothing but be quiet in his presence—and I come out with a deep peace. Sometimes I'll get some thought or insight and sometimes I won't; but I always get peace. So that would be my relationship with Christ. However, when I'm talking in prayer, having a conversation, it will be with his mother. Maybe I should examine my conscience and see if I'm spending too much time with Mary and not enough time with Jesus!

• • •**Q**   *How do you nurture and express your relationship with Jesus?*

• • •**A**   I do it by picking a word every day from the liturgy. At the Mass, I take a word from the Gospel and listen to what it says to me. Otherwise, it's so easy to go to my favorite Scriptures all the time. You know, I'd be stuck with: "The Lord is my shepherd," "God, you know me and you probe me," "Seek the Lord while he may be found." Everyone has their favorite Scripture passages, and we tend to avoid the ones we're not comfortable with. So I make it a rule to study the Scripture for the Mass of the day and confine myself to one word. Then, at night, I examine my conscience on that word. For example, today my word is "restoration." Now, I've been to confession today, I've been restored. That's how I try to live the word. Tonight I'll say, "Yes Lord, I needed to be restored, I've been restored, I've lived the word."

• • •**Q**   *Do you have any form of prayer that you use the most?*

• • •**A**   I was very much into the centering prayer, or
"prayer of the heart" as it is sometimes called. But as
my prayer life is deepening I'd say my favorite prayer is
the Rosary. One of the things that I do, which may be a
little bit different, is that I don't just say the Rosary, but
I take the Joyful mysteries and try to feel what Mary
felt. In the Sorrowful mysteries, I ask Jesus, how did he
feel in the garden? I try to imagine what it must have
been like to sweat blood or to be crowned with thorns,
or scourged, to carry the cross.... The Glorious mysteries
I find the most difficult, so I think about how the early
Christians felt at those moments. To me the Joyful
mysteries are the feelings of Mary, the Sorrowful mysteries are the feelings of Christ, and the Glorious mysteries are the feelings of the Church, especially the early
Church.

• • •**Q**   *The Rosary has had its ups and downs...but you
can't throw out something that is proven to be good, can you?*

• • •**A**   It's incredible...the Rosary almost disappeared,
and now it's the hottest selling item! When I give a
retreat to young people, I invariably finish up by teaching them how to pray the Rosary. In the last session I
ask them to share the high point, or turning point of the
retreat. Ninety percent report it was learning about the
Rosary.

• • •**Q**   *Do you do a lot of work with youth?*

• • •**A**   Mostly. Yes, the biggest part of my work is
with youth.

• • •**Q**   *Why do you draw a lot of youth?*

• • •**A**   Maybe because I'm English! I think English
things attract—the accent, the playboy part of my life—
it helps to attract these young people.

• • •**Q**   *So you're comfortable speaking to the young?*

• • •**A**   More comfortable with them than with the adults.

• • •**Q**   *What would you say to a smorgasbord Catholic?*

• • •**A**   There was a time in my more liberal days when I tried to be all things to all people. I wanted to please people, and when you do that you soon discover that you've pleased no one...especially not yourself. Now I try to please God alone. I find that especially in the confessional. Some people try to intimidate the priest by saying, "You know, Father, I don't believe this is a sin! I practice contraception, but I don't believe it's a sin." So I ask them, "Then why are you confessing it?" "Well, I want your opinion." I continue with that line of questioning and am told that my opinion is sought because I'm a priest. I remind them that John Paul II is a priest, and ask why they'd consider my opinion over his. I remind them that John Paul II's opinion is a teaching. Now, I wouldn't have done that years ago, but I do now. Years ago, I thought: don't rock the boat. Today I'm convinced that I must be compassionate where compassion is needed, but I cannot be compassionate when a person is unrepentant, or insolent, or arrogant—because with arrogance there's no repentance. The same thing applies to absolution.... I don't baptize someone who doesn't want to be Catholic, and I can't absolve someone who's not repentant. So we've got to bring people to repentance.

• • •**Q**   *Do you think people really want an easy way out?*

• • •**A**   No, especially not young people. In fact, one time at Medjugorje a young person really shook me up. He was about nineteen years old and came to confession—his second confession since his First Communion.

He had a lot to confess, and I was trying to be very compassionate, with the hope that it would be a wonderful experience for him. I gave him a very light penance and he said, "Father, that's not a penance." I said, "Well, that's all you have to do." He answered, "I want a real penance. I made a real confession, so give me a real penance...one I'll never forget." So I told him to climb Mount Crucibex, barefoot. And he was happy about that.

• • •**Q**   *Incredible! Is there anything else you'd like to add, Father?*

• • •**A**   I'd like to stress that sometimes it's so easy to be negative.... Sure, there are problems in today's Church—but the Church has gone through worse and has survived. It's going through a bad time now, but I think it's being purified and pruned. To me, Vatican II was a pruning, and after the pruning it looks pretty ugly. But I think there's going to be a fantastic crop of saints in the next generation. Maybe the greatest crop of saints the Church has ever known.

*Born in Cedarhurst, New York,
Fr. Michael Scanlan, TOR, is both a
lawyer (JD, Harvard Law School,
1956) and a friar-priest. From 1969
to 1974, Fr. Scanlan served as rector
of the St. Francis Seminary in
Loretto, Pennsylvania, and is
currently the president of the
Franciscan University of
Steubenville, Ohio. He is a well-
known author and lecturer.*

MICHAEL SCANLAN, TOR

•••**Q** *Father, you're a lawyer, a friar-priest active in the Charismatic Renewal, and president of a dynamic university, how do you picture Jesus? Is there a particular image of the Lord that comes to your mind in prayer?*

•••**A** There's no particular picture, but there's a sense of presence, of encounter, a sense at times of touching or grasping on to him. It's more like I'm in Jesus rather than he's in me...it varies, and is a real personal contact. During prayer itself I seldom picture anything, but when I begin my prayer I frequently picture Jesus at prayer.

•••**Q** *Where do you picture Jesus at prayer? In the Garden of Olives, the Upper Room...?*

•••**A** Well, I've seen the movie *Jesus of Nazareth* so many times that when I begin prayer I frequently picture Jesus in one of those scenes—like when he's praying all night long and the apostles are sleeping.

•••**Q** *And what about Jesus' personality or character... how would you describe Jesus to someone who had never heard of him?*

•••**A** I guess I find Jesus to be all-encompassing. In

other words, he's so much bigger than I am—in character, love, understanding, compassion, truth and insight. It's as if his character and personality encompass, heal and strengthen all those same areas of my life.

• • •**Q**   *When you read the Gospel, which of Christ's words are, for you, the most comforting, challenging...the most relevant?*

• • •**A**   Well, let me say, first, that the words in the New Testament that most frequently jump out at me are actually from the Letter to the Romans: "No longer live as unbelievers do, but be converted by the renewal of your mind so that you can test and approve what God's will is, his good, holy and perfect will" (cf Rom 12:2). Those are, for me, the most challenging words of the Bible. They challenge me to an ongoing conversion of heart and mind. They tell me that my mind needs to be converted, to think as God does, to test and approve God's will. Words that I find comforting are from John 15:7, where Jesus says, "If you abide in me and my word abides in you ask what you will and it will be given to you."

• • •**Q**   *Do you believe that?*

• • •**A**   I thoroughly believe that. And I've found it to be true—as long as I am striving to abide in the Lord, to be rooted in him, surrounded by him, and to take on all the words that he has spoken. To take on and in his words and not reject any of them, but to let them abide in me. Another text that gives me great solace is when Jesus said, "In my Father's house there are many mansions" (cf Jn 14:2). That gives me great comfort in loving and working with others. Why? Because it tells me I don't have to be like them and they don't have to be like me. We all just have to follow the Lord. So I have great delight whenever I find someone zealously trying to follow the Lord, even if he/she is so different from me. It's then that I remember that there are many rooms and many mansions.

• • •Q   *Are those the texts where you feel that the Lord is speaking just for you?*

• • •A   The text I mentioned from Paul to the Romans, "No longer live as unbelievers do..." is something that I believe God has given to me very personally. I feel a particular call in my life to preach repentance. I am convinced that repentance is the door to any blessing in life and to any growth in the spiritual life. In terms of my personal mission, repentance is the key. It is, of course, also in the tradition of my particular branch of the Franciscans, as I belong to the Third Order of St. Francis of Penance. People tell me that in all my books—and I've written a dozen—the sections on repentance are the most powerful.

• • •Q   *Father, in your personal relationship with Jesus, do you have a particular title by which you think of and refer to him?*

• • •A   Jesus is the Master and Teacher who is personally calling me forth, caring for me and training me. The title of Master evokes a sense of endearment and closeness. I feel Jesus leads his band of disciples (and I'm one of them), and I can call him Lord and Master not only as a term of sovereignty, but in terms of intimacy and endearment.

• • •Q   *When did this relationship with Jesus become a significant part of your life? Was it always there, or can you point to a moment when you became truly aware of it?*

• • •A   My relationship with Christ went through

various stages. I was given the gift of faith on my nineteenth birthday. I asked for it, and I got it: the gift of a general faith in God, the Scriptures and the Church. But my relationship to Christ was not yet personal. Then, in my first year at the Harvard Law School, I encountered the Lord in a spiritual experience. One day, in 1954, while coming back from morning Mass, I knew there was a personal call on my life and that God could personally speak to me. Then, in 1965, while making a Cursillo Retreat, I developed a relationship with Jesus that centered on his very person. The last stage (but there never is a last stage), was in 1969, when I was baptized in the Holy Spirit. Then my relationship became one with the Resurrected Lord Jesus, who is present in my life with love and power.

• • •**Q** *Would you say, then, that each stage brought a deeper intimacy with the Lord?*

• • •**A** Definitely! In each stage the relationship became more personal, intimate and powerful. More-over, as I became intimate with the Lord Crucified, I found that my own pain and suffering have increased that intimacy.

• • •**Q** *How does Fr. Michael Scanlan nurture and express his relationship with Jesus? Is there a special type of prayer that you practice?*

• • •**A** Spending substantial prayer time in the morn-ing is the key to my life...submitting to the Lord every-thing I'm going to do that day before I go off and do it.

• • •**Q** *What form does that morning prayer take?*

• • •**A** I wrote a book called *Appointment with God*. It's about a basic approach to prayer which I myself follow. It's based on first proclaiming who God is, praising him and focusing my life in that direction. Then seeking God's revelation through the words of Scripture or from the readings of the day in the Office. Then taking the word, feeding on it, dwelling on it, and being present to the Lord through the freshness of that revelation—even though it may be words of Scripture that I've prayed many times. And then I look to see how it would apply to my life in terms of changing my life, and writing down in my journal what I need to do differently or understand better. Then I move to confident intercession for what I need and what the people who are in my care need. Finally, I write down some resolutions about the day's agenda. I do that daily, along with some communal morning prayer with the brothers, and it always takes a couple of hours to complete.

• • •Q   *Would you share one or two other personal spiritual experiences with the Lord?*

• • •A   The one that's foremost in my mind is an experience of the Virgin Mary, who was assuring me that my mother was with her in heaven; that experience has had such an impact on my life. It occurred during an apparition in Medjugorje. I was kneeling next to the visionaries, and I had a tremendous, absolute certainty that Mary was telling me that my own mother was right there with her. You see, my mother had lived most of her life in a divorced-remarried state...although in the last part of her life she had been very fervent. There was something so real about that experience at Medjugorje that it has given me enormous hope and pierced me through and through.

The other experience was of the Lord Jesus Christ, in 1965, when I was sure I was going to crash in a Piper Cub. We were caught in a hail storm and I figured I had only a few minutes to live. I turned to the Lord in prayer and said, "There are many things in my life which I wish I hadn't done...and there are many things that I wish I had done...I'm sorry! I trust you with everything and with whatever is left of my life!" And I had such an experience of peace, light, hope and the presence of the Lord that I didn't care whether the plane crashed or not. I have never forgotten that moment. The Lord's mercy and forgiveness are so great, they envelop you. I felt like the good thief being told, "This day you'll be with me in paradise." Those two experiences have stayed with me the longest.

• • •**Q** *If Jesus came back to earth today, what would you want him to speak about on prime time television? What topic do you think would be the most beneficial for people to hear about?*

• • •**A** Heaven!

• • •**Q** *Heaven?*

• • •**A** People have to get their eyes focused on where they're going to live forever.

• • •**Q** *So, I guess you'd want him to reassure us that it is real and worth struggling for?*

• • •**A** Yes, and of the tremendous reality of it—filled with people. And that there are people there whom we know; and of the Lord's desire to have us come home to heaven.

John Michael Talbot is known throughout the world as a musician, author and preacher who proclaims Jesus Christ through his music, writings and lifestyle. He is the founder and current superior general of the Brothers and Sisters of Charity, a canonically erected, integrated monastic community of celibates and of families who live an evangelical life of consecration. John Michael currently resides at the Little Portion hermitage in Eureka Springs, Arkansas.

JOHN MICHAEL TALBOT

•••Q *John Michael, how do you picture Jesus when you pray?*

•••A Well, I remember going to Sunday school as a little boy, in the Methodist Church, and doing all the Sunday school things—playing games and having bible verse quizzes. But the pictures on the wall are what really stay with me: Jesus the Good Shepherd, Jesus at the Sermon on the Mount.... I remember intuiting, even as a child, something in those pictures that is beyond words, something very solid, comforting and gentle. Franco Zeferelli has probably captured better than anyone else my image of Jesus—the Jesus in his *Jesus of Nazareth* has, for me, an utterly compelling face; that image resonates with me.

•••Q *Does your perception of Jesus affect your music?*

•••A Well, it is said of Michelangelo that he knew God had put an image into the materials he was working with—stone, marble, etc.—and that it was his job only to uncover it. If he went too far he would do damage to the material rather than help the image's release. I have the same sense about my music. When I am writing a song, singing, recording, producing an album, I have the sense that God has already put that music into my head and heart, and it definitely comes from Jesus. My job is to uncover what God has already given me. When I write a song, I know when it's finished and I know when it's time to stop. If I go further I would begin to do an injustice to what God has given me. When writing music, performing or producing a beautiful work of art, there's a point where you know that Jesus is there, but you can go beyond him or back away from him.

• • •**Q** *Is there a recent experience in which your perception of Jesus has been touched in a special way?*

• • •**A** I guess the immediate thing that comes to mind is my marriage. My relationship with Viola has brought an immediacy of human contact that has opened up my heart. Celibacy was an incredible gift in my life, and there may again be times when I will live as a celibate. But I have found that my marriage to Viola brought a human being close enough into my orbit that I had to be challenged: Am I really being Jesus? Am I really meeting this human conflict and working through it? Or am I just running back to my cell, my hermitage, or my room, and praying and getting involved in a bunch of "Jesus things," without really dealing with various aspects of my own heart? Viola challenges me to pray more, to be more loving, not to become complacent about certain things that, in monastic solitude, I can easily become complacent about. I would say that my marriage to Viola has definitely brought me to Jesus in a whole new way—a wonderful way.

• • •**Q** *And, when you are at prayer in your cell or with the community, how do you perceive Jesus' personality?*

• • •A Whole, balanced, incredible strength and incredible gentleness all at once. I often say that Jesus is the truth. A lot of us can speak the truth without wisdom, and a lot of us can be loving but not be wise in our love. To me, Jesus is the incarnation of God's wisdom as well as his truth.

• • •Q *When did your relationship with Jesus become a meaningful part of your life?*

• • •A There was an actual conversion experience when I was seventeen years old. I prayed, "God who are you?" I prayed that for over a year. And one day I looked up out of my prayer, and there was an image of Jesus—a typical Christ figure, robed in white. At that point, as a young man, I began calling myself a Christian, although theologically I didn't really know what that meant. As a fundamentalist, evangelical charismatic, I had a kind of Christian certainty. I was sure I had all the answers to all the world's problems. And, wow! did I get busted up. Then I began to discover the deeper dimension of Christianity—the brokenness that really brings the beauty of the Lord into the foreground of one's life.

• • •Q *John Michael, if Jesus were to come back to earth today and speak on prime time TV, what topic would you like him to speak about?*

• • •A Selfless love! If he were to speak on prime time television in America, I would like him to speak about a love that is selfless. Why? Because, without a doubt, as a society, we've become very self-preoccupied.

• • •Q *When you read through the Gospels, what words of Jesus seem to be the most challenging or most comforting?*

• • •A I find Matthew 23 to be the most challenging: Jesus upbraiding the scribes and pharisees—because today all who are followers of Jesus easily become scribes and pharisees. But when I heard you say "comforting," my immediate thought was "blessed"—as in "Blessed are you..." from the Sermon on the Mount. But that's also challenging because I'm not always doing what Jesus says will be blessed. So, sometimes I am the scribe and the pharisee, but sometimes I am also one of the poor who are called blessed, those who mourn, those who sorrow.

• • •**Q** *When you read Scripture, in which text do you feel our Lord is speaking directly to you, John Michael Talbot?*

• • •**A** "Come unto me, all of you who are weary and find life burdensome and I will refresh you, for my yoke is easy and my burden is light" (cf Mt 11:28-29). That's the one for me. Even life in a monastery—maybe especially there—can be stress filled. You know, you get into a community and life becomes very immediate, and relationships with twenty-five other people become very immediate. Out in the world there was a lot of stress, but, you know, your Christian life doesn't have to be very immediate—you don't have to reveal a lot of yourself on Sunday morning, or at the Wednesday night prayer meeting.... When you're living with other people in a community, the "face" kind of melts away under the heat of reality.

• • •**Q** *And now, here you are, living a rather austere life in a monastic community. Who is Jesus for you today?*

• • •**A** We desperately need to understand that Jesus isn't just a right theology, a correct morality, or a good prayer life. And while all those things are good, Christianity centers on the *person* of Jesus. Here in our community we have made a commitment to have daily exposition and adoration of the Blessed Sacrament. We are there on our knees before the Blessed Sacrament—no words, no sermon, no singing, no prophesying. And God has worked incredible miracles in our hearts; in our community and in our hearts a transformation has happened. I know that some people today say that the Eucharist is meant to be received and not adored—and I guess there are many theological arguments about that—but I know that when we got on our knees, and didn't say a word, Jesus was there. Miracles began to happen.

• • •Q *John Michael, when you're in prayer before the Blessed Sacrament, what names or titles of Jesus come to you?*

• • •A To me the word "Jesus" is all-inclusive. But beyond any titles, my desire is to sit at his feet and soak him in.

• • •Q *How do you do that? How do you nurture your personal relationship with Jesus?*

• • •A I nurture that relationship through prayer and meditation, and by trying to do the things that I do normally in my life with Jesus. When I make the time to do the little things—like going out and digging in a garden, or doing the manual work to be done around the monastery—I'm humbled, and I'm brought back to a humble relationship with Christ.

Another area that nurtures my relationship with Jesus is when I go out and do street ministry, talking to people who will never come to a concert, never buy a record or book. When I do that kind of nitty-gritty, hands on, almost invisible ministry, it nurtures my relationship with Jesus in a way that is indescribable.

*Long-time memeber of the Charis-
matic Renewal, Barbara Thorp is
wife, mother, author and lecturer.
She is currently the director of the
Pro-Life Office of the Archdiocese of
Boston and coordinator of Project
Rachel.*

BARBARA THORP

• • •Q *Barbara, when you think of Jesus, do you get a particular visual picture of him? When you pray, are there any images of Jesus that come to mind?*

• • •A I don't have a visual image, but I do have a sense of a joy-filled person. Movies never seem to depict Jesus with a sense of humor, but I sense in him a range of human emotions, particularly humor and joy.

• • •Q *What about Jesus' personality? What makes him attractive or appealing...?*

• • •A I find his qualities of unconditional love and welcome, no matter what condition we're in, particularly attractive. I love his sensitive insight into people— his respect and love even for those living sinful lives. One of my favorite Scriptures is about the woman at the well. Jesus must have smiled as he conversed with her. I have the impression that Jesus said, "I'll take you as you are, but I am going to challenge you a little bit. I'm just not going to leave you where you were." There's more, there's that pull, that call—but we're the ones who have to take the step, nothing is forced.

• • •Q *Is that your favorite scene from the Gospels? Are there others that really speak to you?*

• • •**A**   That is one of my favorites—it shows how Jesus has a way of moving people to another level without clobbering them or destroying them. I don't want to call it gentle, but it's sensitive. One thing I like about John Paul's document *On the Dignity of Women* is the way it puts together and highlights all the Gospel stories about women. Those stories have always sustained me because all those women were, in a way, at all different levels in terms of their faith life. But Jesus knew with each one how to nurture and bring them forward. And sometimes maybe we are like Mary Magdalene, or like Elizabeth.... Jesus really made a point of having women as part of his life and ministry. The Lord really does invite us to be in relationship to him in all kinds of ways.

• • •**Q**   *And in your personal relationship with Jesus, do you think of him mostly as a healer, teacher, rescuer...?*

• • •**A**   He is all of that for me, but I think the constant thing is guide. None of the words I can come up with are adequate—they all seem to fall short of what I really want to say—and guide doesn't really capture it either. Maybe it's Jesus as *Way.*

• • •**Q**   *Barbara, when did you first have an awareness of your relationship with Jesus?*

• • •**A**   Well, there are different levels of awareness. Probably the earliest would be as a child—I had a real sense of God's presence. I remember the Sister at school (it must have been in first or second grade) saying that we must be aware of how much we have been given, how many opportunities we have. And she said that there is some greater good that God will want from us in return. I can remember that moment because I think it was the dawning of a sense of tremendous gratitude to God for the gifts that he has given to me. He's just been incredibly generous.

Another level of awareness comes from my work and relationship with people who have gone through great sorrow or pain—I've been spared much of what they suffer. And I know that God has given me so much—so many opportunities, nurturing, positive moments—that I must be a good steward of those gifts, a channel of God's love. I try to live that way, but I don't always live up to it. Stewardship is always at the back of my mind.

• • • Q *You know, about two months ago my confessor spoke to me about stewardship. He told me to be humble with my gifts and to handle them with careful gratitude. It was as if I heard those words for the first time, and all the lights inside of me went on.*

• • • A Yes, we all have certain qualities and other people comment on them—to our embarrassment. But maybe, instead of being embarrassed, we should try to see what others see. Accept our gifts and make them more beautiful and attractive, so that we can be all that God wants us to be, so that God can use us for his purposes.

• • • Q *Would you share with me an experience of when Christ was personally present to you?*

• • • A Eleven years ago I had one of the most extraordinary experiences of God's presence in my life—it was on the first day of my pregnancy. For a long time David and I had been trying to conceive a child, but nothing happened. One evening we went out to the Gospel Center in Waltham, on the fifth night of a Charismatic seminar, and we were praying for an outpouring of the Holy Spirit on those who had been participating in it.

While we were praying, I became suddenly aware of a tremendous heat within my whole pelvic area. It was as if I was on fire, and I knew something special was happening. David was next to me and I told him that I knew we had conceived. He looked puzzled, and I asked him to trust me. So we kept praying and the heat within me continued to burn. It was a singular experience! Eventually, we had Catherine, our beautiful daughter.

• • •**Q**   *That's incredible! What do you think was the meaning of an experience like that?*

• • •**A**   As time went on, I just accepted it as a grace from God and didn't think more about it. Well, about five years later I was praying about it, and I asked God what it was all about. Why had he allowed me to have such a truly extraordinary experience? And slowly, in answer to my prayer, I came to understand that God had allowed me the grace to physically experience a new life coming into being, but that this experience was not unique to me. In other words, this experience of God's presence at conception is true for every woman who conceives—the difference was that God had allowed me to have a physical sense, a total awareness, that it was happening.

• • •**Q**   *Is that why you became so committed to the pro-life work?*

• • •**A**   Well, prior to that experience, I had never really thought about the abortion issue. But, as soon as the Lord gave me that insight into his role in procreation, my immediate thought was about abortion. It all became clear, and I knew that, because of my experience, God was really asking me to get involved with the pro-life work. Well, I began to pray and think about it. I explored a number of different possibilities, from joining Birth Right to doing some volunteer work. Then, I read about Project Rachel, and I knew that I should get more information about it. I still didn't know what my role was to be, but I began to make some initial inquiries within the Archdiocese about it.

•••Q *Had Project Rachel been implemented here in Boston yet?*

•••A No. But I knew that women were carrying tremendous sorrow and tremendous pain as a result of past abortions, and I began to mention Project Rachel to different people. I spoke about it to my boss at Catholic Charities and he was touched and moved by it. The word went up the chain a bit, and I had a sense that I had now done my part. Then one day I had a call from Cardinal Law, asking me if I'd direct a full-time Pro-life Office in the Archdiocese. I couldn't believe it! I said yes with one proviso...that the first thing I could do was to implement Project Rachel.

•••Q *Why did Project Rachel catch your interest?*

•••A Project Rachel really touched me because I saw the need for [spiritual and emotional] healing—so many women are hurt and have been drawn into abortions without fully realizing what they were doing. I think many clergy particularly welcomed Project Rachel as a vehicle through which they could reach out and talk about God's mercy and love, a means to tell people that there's a way back for them.

•••Q *Jesus must be an important part of your work; how do you keep your relationship with Jesus alive?*

•••A Because of my many obligations, I can't always set aside an hour every day for prayer and Scripture; it just doesn't happen that way in my life. I wouldn't be honest if I said it did. But I find the Jesus Prayer very sustaining, and I use it as a backdrop. With it, there's an awareness and a seeking of God's mercy, and an awareness of how much I'm in need of his mercy and love. It helped me when I worked with the elderly and I saw so many who were being abused. And it helps me when talking with women who have had abortions. All the pain and sorrow—especially with abortion—is so profound, the ache and hurt so deep, that you can't help but just be aware of the depth God's mercy, of how much God loves these women and their aborted children.

• • •**Q**   *Barbara, it sounds as if you connect with a lot of people in their pain....*

• • •**A**   Yes, and it's always a moment of grace for me when I talk with these pain-filled women. Women do share their feelings more easily than men, but it is still rare for women to talk easily about abortion. It's not something that you sit down and chat about with your friends or sisters. So when these women call, for many of them it's the first opportunity they've had to talk with another woman about something that they've been carrying deep within them, unexpressed and unable to be shared with anyone. That always puts me in touch with the greatness of God's love, mercy, and grace, and how we—all of us—are in need of it.

• • •**Q**   *That is so true, but aren't there many women who simply cannot forgive themselves?*

• • •**A**   There's no question that for many women their sin seems bigger than God and his mercy. And some cannot even imagine that their aborted child can forgive them. For me, even greater than the sin of abortion is the evil endured by the person who is convinced that God doesn't love them and can't forgive them. That conviction is Satan's greatest triumph. Abortion itself was a great sin, but to keep that person in bondage to the sin by his/her inability to accept God's love, because their sin seems bigger than God, that is a great evil. And I know this to be true, because those women who do accept God's forgiveness, love and mercy are so set free of the bondage of sin, that because of their experience they can go out and free others. They are alive with the love of God and do so much good.

Director of the Office of Evangelization for the Archdiocese of Boston,
David Thorp is a graduate of Boston
College with degrees in psychology
and theology. Since 1971 he has
been actively involved with the
Catholic Charismatic Renewal.

DAVID THORP

●●●**Q** *David, with your work in evangelization, and your involvement in the Charismatic Renewal, who is the person of Jesus for you?*

●●●**A** It changes, but I do have two traditional devotions: to the Sacred Heart and to the Holy Names. I developed the Holy Names devotion about five years ago—I pray a litany of the titles or the attributes of the Lord starting at A and going to Z. It's a way of focusing by using my mind in prayer. Right now the focus is on Jesus as "Incarnate Word." Jesus is the Word made flesh, God who became human.

●●●**Q** *At prayer do you have a mental picture of Jesus?*

●●●**A** Sometimes I do. The picture of Jesus that I see most is of him squatting—like somebody in a marketplace. You wouldn't stand there all day, with tiredness you would squat. I see Jesus in that position, watching people, open to them. Squatting is a Middle Eastern or Asian thing. People can squat all day long, it's as if they're saying with their bodies, "Here we are."

●●●**Q** *What does his face look like?*

●●●**A** Dark complexion, stringy hair, not nicely

coiffured. And he's dirty—his feet are dirty, his robes grayish white—but he's always smiling, as if he knows something that you don't know. It's a smile of invitation and welcome.

• • •**Q**   *What kind of inviting characteristics or personality traits do you see in Jesus?*

• • •**A**   The characteristic that I find most inviting is his inclusion. No one is excluded from this guy. He includes everything, yet, he manages to turn everything upside down. He shows us what it means to say things like "Teacher." "You call me teacher? OK. I'll wash your feet!" Or, "You want me to be merciful? Yes. I'll show you what mercy really means...." Wow! Lord, you take me in, and then you change the way I view teacher, Lord, master, God. You change all that.

• • •**Q**   *That sounds like a very open minded Jesus; yet Jesus is seen by many as one who made a lot of rules that are difficult to follow. Have we pinned the wrong thing on Jesus?*

• • •**A**   I'm not sure that he made a lot of rules that are difficult to follow. I think he said some very simple things, easy things, things that model his inclusion. Jesus was a guy who was fully alive. I think of Jesus as being very self-assured, having a self-confidence that came from knowing who he was. And from that knowledge he says, "This is who I am. And I think the incredible thing is, this is who *you* are. I'm the Son of God, and *you* are the son or daughter of God. What I have by nature, you have by grace." And for me, that's the amazing thing. Jesus has this incredibly intimate relationship with the Father by nature, and we have it by grace, we have it as a gift. So when he gives these rules, he's basically saying, "You can do this. Everything that I said, you can do."

• • •Q   *When you read the words of Jesus from the Gospels, are there any parts which seem to speak just to you?*

• • •A   Yes, Matthew 11, where Jesus says, "Come to me, all who are heavily laden, my burden is easy, be yoked to me." It sounds like he's telling us we have to do something, I hear that part. But I also hear the implication that on his part he is willing to be yoked to us—tied to our condition. He says, "I want to be yoked to you...so, be yoked to me." Again, it's not a rule, a regulation or requirement. It's the Lord saying, "This is how we can be together." I find that to be a great consolation.

• • •Q   *Any more favorite texts?*

• • •A   Yes, Romans 5:8, wherein we see God as an impatient lover! God can't wait for us to get our act together. God said, "Forget it, I'm going to grasp you, in the midst of your sin, alienation, brokenness. That's when I love you." The impatient love of God!

• • •Q   *How do you continue to nurture and express your relationship with Jesus?*

• • •A   I'm nurtured by the Scriptures, in private prayer, by spiritual friends who are able to tell me when I'm on or off base. And of course the Eucharist—I think I understand about five percent of what the Eucharist is all about. And every time I receive the Eucharist, I pray, "Lord, just let me understand this five percent, please, five percent." You see, if I would just understand five percent my life could be completely different. The Eucharist is what keeps the fire going for me.

• • •Q   *Do you use any particular prayer method? Is there one that you're more comfortable with?*

• • •A   Right now prayer doesn't come as easily as it

did before. That used to bother me, but it doesn't any-more. I've tried spontaneous prayer with great fervor and dedication. I use the Divine Office, and I keep saying that maybe if I continue with it for five years it will wash over me...but it hasn't yet. I can begin with Psalm 95, that kind of lets me leap in, then from there it's very spontaneous prayers of praise and intercession. And I make use of the Scriptures. I like praying over the daily readings from the Mass. It's marvelous to know that I'm connected with all these other people—here's God's word for me, God's word for nine hundred million Catholics today.

• • •Q   *How do you find time for prayer in a schedule as busy as yours?*

• • •A   We pray frequently at our office—we take time from our "work time" for prayer. I pray better with others, it's much easier for me when I'm gathered with a community of persons, even though the prayer is very private and individual. And I am definitely a "night pray-er." You know, I like it when there's only one light on in the whole house, and it's the place where I am. There's something comforting and also something challenging about the darkness.

• • •Q   *Have there been any special experiences when Jesus touched your life in a more tangible way?*

• • •A   I can taste one every day, I really think I can. But, let me tell you about February, 1981. I was praying with a group of friends and in my mind I could see the Lord with his back to me, dancing on a hill. When he turned around he was smiling. It was a wonderful invitation...he opened his arms, his cloak fell open, and there was a huge gash in his side. Then I heard words similar to those spoken to St. Thomas. Our Lord said to me, "David, step inside!" And in my mind's eye I watched myself approach the Lord. I took one of my legs and put it inside the Lord, then I wiggled in my shoulder, then my other leg.... And there I was, sitting in the belly of the Lord! I could hear his heart beat, I could hear him breathing. Immediately, the Scripture verse, "In him we live, we move, we have our being" (cf Acts 17:28) became a reality. I experienced the Lord's presence, knowing that's where I belong. I belong in the belly of the Lord. I am to be immersed in him. It's not just that God lives in me through the wonder of the Eucharist, but I can live in God. I'm in God; he's in me. Jesus is in the Father; I'm in the Father. We're all united.

• • •**Q** *Given our world and its many problems, what is it that you'd like Jesus to do to help us open our eyes?*

• • •**A** I'm not sure that he could do anything in a big flashy way. But if he was here to speak, I think people need to know that they are loved! We need to know that there is this love from which we cannot be separated except by our own choosing. We need to understand that if we want to walk away from that love we can, but God's love is always there. I would want him to tell us about his unconditional love for us. Somehow I have the idea that if he said it we'd believe it—because he has the ability to read people's thoughts and to pierce through their hearts. His message wouldn't be big and complicated, it would be, "This is who you are, and you're accepted and loved!" That's what I'd want him to say.

St. Paul Book & Media Centers

ALASKA
  750 West 5th Ave., Anchorage, AK 99501 907-272-8183.
CALIFORNIA
  3908 Sepulveda Blvd., Culver City, CA 90230 310-397-8676.
  1570 Fifth Ave. (at Cedar Street), San Diego, CA 92101 619-232-1442
  46 Geary Street, San Francisco, CA 94108 415-781-5180.
FLORIDA
  145 S.W. 107th Ave., Miami, FL 33174 305-559-6715; 305-559-6716.
HAWAII
  1143 Bishop Street, Honolulu, HI 96813 808-521-2731.
ILLINOIS
  172 North Michigan Ave., Chicago, IL 60601 312-346-4228; 312-346-3240.
LOUISIANA
  4403 Veterans Memorial Blvd., Metairie, LA 70006 504-887-7631; 504-887-0113.
MASSACHUSETTS
  50 St. Paul's Ave., Jamaica Plain, Boston, MA 02130 617-522-8911.
  Rte. 1, 885 Providence Hwy., Dedham, MA 02026 617-326-5385.
MISSOURI
  9804 Watson Rd., St. Louis, MO 63126 314-965-3512; 314-965-3571.
NEW JERSEY
  561 U.S. Route 1, Wick Plaza, Edison, NJ 08817 908-572-1200.
NEW YORK
  150 East 52nd Street, New York, NY 10022 212-754-1110.
  78 Fort Place, Staten Island, NY 10301 718-447-5071; 718-447-5086.
OHIO
  2105 Ontario Street (at Prospect Ave.), Cleveland, OH 44115 216-621-9427.
PENNSYLVANIA
  214 W. DeKalb Pike, King of Prussia, PA 19406 215-337-1882; 215-337-2077.
SOUTH CAROLINA
  243 King Street, Charleston, SC 29401 803-577-0175.
TEXAS
  114 Main Plaza, San Antonio, TX 78205 512-224-8101.
VIRGINIA
  1025 King Street, Alexandria, VA 22314 703-549-3806.
CANADA
  3022 Dufferin Street, Toronto, Ontario, Canada M6B 3T5 416-781-9131.